# Online Operator

## About The Author.

Bernard Kamoroff is a Certified Public Accountant with over twenty years' experience, specializing in small business. Mr. Kamoroff has worked directly with hundreds of businesses, and has been a guest speaker at business and trade association meetings and conventions.

He has given business workshops and seminars for the University of California, American River College, Mendocino College, The Open Exchange, Learning Annex, and San Francisco Business Renaissance.

Books by Bernard Kamoroff include:

**Small Time Operator:** How to Start Your Own Business,
    Keep Your Books, Pay Your Taxes & Stay Out of Trouble.
**422 Tax Deductions** for Businesses and Self Employed Individuals.
**We Own It:** Starting & Managing Employee Owned Businesses.
**Small Time Operator: The Software**.

In addition to helping other businesses, Mr. Kamoroff has started and successfully operated three of his own small businesses.

Bernard Kamoroff makes his home in Mendocino County, California. He can be reached c/o Bell Springs Publishing, Box 1240, Willits, California 95490; or Kamoroff@bellsprings.com.

# Online Operator
## Business, Legal, and Tax
## Guide to the Internet

Bernard Kamoroff, C.P.A.

BELL
SPRINGS
Publishing

Willits & Laytonville, California

Published by
## BELL SPRINGS PUBLISHING
Box 1240, Willits, California 95490
telephone 707/459-6372    fax 707/459-8614
e-mail: publisher@bellsprings.com
www.bellsprings.com

### First Edition
Library of Congress Catalog Number 2001-1089164
ISBN: 0-917510-20-8

Man and cart illustration by Bruce McCloskey.
Computer in cart courtesy of Patty Walsh, And Books.
Home office design courtesy of Linda Blair Design, Scarsdale, N.Y.
Title typeface, and text illustrations designed by
Eric Hoggatt, Presstige Graphics, Willits, California
Chapter 21, "When Your Web Site Goes Down," courtesy of
Tom Person, Laughing Bear Newsletter, Box 613322, Dallas TX 75261

The illustration of the man and the cart, and the Bell Springs logo are
trademarks of Bell Springs Publishing.

**Quantity Purchases:**
We offer substantial discounts on bulk sales to organizations, schools, professionals, and businesses. More information, call (707) 459-6372.

**Please Read:**
I have done my best to give you useful, accurate information in this book, but I cannot guarantee that the information is correct or will be appropriate to your situation. Laws and regulations change frequently and are subject to differing interpretations. It is your responsibility to verify all information and laws discussed in this book before relying on them. Nothing in this book can substitute for legal advice and cannot be considered as making it unnecessary to obtain such advice.

# Keeping Current

The Internet is moving constantly, and the regulators are moving right along with it. Online Operator is revised and updated every printing. If you are reading an older edition of this book, be careful to verify any legal and tax information to be sure it is still current.

## Annual Update Sheet

To help you keep up with the business, tax, and legal changes affecting Internet business, every January we publish a one-page *"Online Operator Update."* If you would like a copy of the Update, send a self-addressed, stamped #10 envelope (business size) and $1.00 to: Online Update, Box 1240, Willits, CA 95490.

## New Edition Offer

We offer a 25% discount off the purchase price of a new edition if you turn in the title page of any earlier edition.

## E-Mail Newsletter

If you would like to receive our free e-mail newsletter, which includes update information for all of our books, send your e-mail address to newsletter@bellsprings.com. (Subscribers to our newsletter will not be added to any mail lists.)

## Questions?

If you have any questions, suggestions, or comments about *Online Operator*, please send them to Bernard Kamoroff, c/o Bell Springs Publishing, PO Box 1240, Willits, California 95490. Or e-mail Kamoroff@bellsprings.com.

## Special Thanks To:

**James Dillehay**, author of "Basic Guide to Selling Crafts on the Internet" (www.craftmarketer.com), for many hours of help, advice, suggestions, and support. There are few people I would label a true "expert" on the Internet and on Web sites; James is among the best.

**Tom Person**, of Laughing Bear Newsletter, for Web site advice and for allowing me to excerpt from the newsletter.

**Eric Hoggatt**, of Presstige Graphics, for all the graphic help.

**Kirk Kroh**, for teaching me Internet programming


## This book is dedicated to my family:

**Crystal Rose**, for the original design work that got this book from an idea into reality.

**Julia**, for making the track team.

**Colleen** and **Corrina**, for getting me out to play basketball.

And especially to **Sharon**. *Some kind of love never dies.*

# Contents

## Section Four: E-Commerce

## Section Five: Law of the Internet

## Section Six: Intellectual Property

## Section Seven: International Commerce

## Section Eight: Home Business

## We've Only Just Begun

## Government Web Addresses

## Index

# Section One:
# The Internet

# Chapter 1:
# Welcome to the Internet Age

*"Things are happening right now. There are lots of people doing things for the first time."*
**—Thomas Dalton, Founder, USBid.com**

There was a time, one hundred years ago, when only a few businesses had a telephone. There was a time, twenty years ago, when only a few businesses had a computer. There was a time, maybe since the last time you went to the dentist, when only a few businesses were on the Internet.

Today, there are 32 million Web sites on the Internet. Half of those Web sites are owned by businesses in the United States. And over 80% of those business sites—over 12 million Web sites—are small businesses, self-employed individuals, independent professionals, and freelancers, many of them one-person and home-based operations.

Brand new businesses are being started and operated 100% on the Internet. No store, no shop, no public visibility, but genuine and successful businesses just the same, providing a product or a service, marketed and sold entirely on the Internet.

Small local businesses are getting national and international customers from the Internet. Established "bricks and mortar" businesses (businesses with a physical location in the real world) are using the Internet to increase visibility and sales. Clicks-and-mortar or bricks-and-clicks ("clicks" referring to using a mouse to click this or that button on a Web site) are common terms given to businesses with both a physical and an Internet presence.

Mail-order businesses are adding the Internet as one more "channel" to reach their customers. Catalog businesses are using the Internet to display their products. Full color catalogs, often prohibitively expensive when printed on paper, are very inexpensive on the Internet. You can change products, prices, and descriptions—and correct mistakes—instantly. Your catalog never has to be out of date when it is on the Net.

Professionals, freelancers, independent contractors, and tradespeople are creating Web sites to communicate with old clients and attract new ones.

Business-to-business (b-to-b) auctions and marketplaces are an inexpensive way to locate new customers, and especially to sell overstock, damaged goods, and outdated merchandise you can no longer sell through your regular business channels. Some business-to-business sites offer barter, where businesses trade goods and services.

eBay and other consumer auction sites have converted thousands of flea market entrepreneurs into Internet entrepreneurs. No more wasted weekends sitting at a booth waiting for bargain-hunters to plunk down their money. List your goods on eBay, scan in a photo, state your minimum bid, and check back in a week. Instead of reaching a couple hundred people on a Sunday afternoon when you'd rather be at the beach, you'll reach thousands of people from all over the country, while you *are* at the beach.

The Internet lets you have multiple businesses, to change businesses on a whim. You can be selling antique typewriters one week, and then switch, overnight, to guitars. Or do both at the same time.

The Internet is especially valuable to businesses that sell unusual products, old and rare items, goods with limited interest. People looking for such goods are usually determined to find them. These people will take the time to search the Internet. If you are on the Net, they will find you.

If you have a specialized niche or esoteric market (such as a business that sells unusual collectibles, or caters to a specialized group of hobbyists, or to people who love a certain breed of animal, or to fans of a certain kind of music, etc.) you can easily make your presence known. By focusing on one very unusual area, you can easily become the specialist, the expert, the place a small but loyal group of customers will return to, and tell others about. This connection between seller and buyer was impossible before the Internet.

The Internet can bring you new business even if you do not have a Web site. Your business can get listed in Internet directories, your products and services can get recommended by Internet sites. If you have a product to sell, you can find other businesses already on the Web that want to offer your product, much like a large catalog might include your products in its pages. You can increase your wholesale business greatly by finding businesses on the Web that might be interested in what you offer.

You can find international markets, overseas customers, and overseas suppliers, something that was time consuming and expensive before the Internet.

## A Word About the Word "Business"

To many people, a "business" is a store, a shop, a manufacturing facility, a warehouse, some physical location selling a physical product.

For this book, and for most books about business, a "business" has a much broader definition. Anyone working for himself or herself is running a business. Self-employed individuals, professionals, independent contractors, free agents, freelance artists and designers may not consider themselves to be "in business." Many, to tell the truth, are often trying to *avoid* business. But owning a business, being in business, running a business, is exactly what they are doing.

You are free to call yourself whatever you like. But if you are self-employed, if you are not on someone else's payroll with withholding and W-2 forms at the end of the year, you are in business for yourself. Everything in this book applies to you. Every reference to "business" applies to you.

I often refer to businesses and self-employed individuals as though they were different things, but they're not, at least for everything you will read in this book.

**Home businesses:** Home-based businesses are no different than out-of-the-home businesses. Although there are a few tax laws and zoning laws that discriminate against home businesses (covered in **Section Eight: Home Businesses**), everything in this book applies equally to all businesses, and to all self-employed individuals, no matter where you are working. Don't let the terminology confuse you.

## "Find a Need and Fill It" on the Internet

"Be Your Own Boss" is the Call of the Wild for most people who decide to start their own business or go independent. These entrepreneurs, business owners, independent professionals, freelancers, free agents, and other self-employed men and women, are usually savvy and creative in their own specialties. But it is easy to get bewildered when facing not only the business rules and regulations people have been facing for years, but also all the new laws and ways of doing business that have developed—and are still being fine-tuned—on the Internet.

A host of possible legal problems await the unprepared business in the Internet environment: internal security risks, domain name disputes, hackers, computer malpractice issues, intellectual property infringement, and an array of online contractual and jurisdictional disputes.

Most business owners don't know their way around these Internet minefields. Fortunately, a safe path is emerging. The cartographers are mapping the new world, and you can now benefit from the lessons learned by the first wave of Internet businesses that ventured out on the uncharted ocean of cyberspace.

Since the beginning of economic time, the first rule of success in any business has been "Find a need and fill it." Two distinct and separate actions. "Find a need." That's where your real genius comes into play. "Fill it." That's what this book will help you to do.

Commerce on the Internet is growing constantly, evolving at a tremendous clip, shedding its old skin before our eyes. As Web tools become more manageable, as the Internet becomes more prevalent, doing business on the Web will become a basic operating skill for most businesses. It's all still very new, but the day is soon coming when the Internet is going to be part of everyday business.

# Chapter 2:
# Introduction to the Internet

*"The borders are coming down, and it is an irreversible trend."*
**—Michael Armstrong, Chairman and CEO, AT&T**

The Internet is a collection of interconnected networks of computers. The computers are connected by telephone lines, fiber optics, earth-based microwave, and orbiting satellites.

The Internet functions because the computer networks that comprise the Internet have agreed on what they call "protocols," pre-agreed on rules and computer languages that govern communications between computers.

## The World Wide Web

Although most people use the terms "Internet" and "World Wide Web" interchangeably, they are not the same. The World Wide Web (the Web) is part of the Internet. Web sites (also called "domains") reside on the World Wide Web and are accessed through the Internet.

Most e-mail, instant messaging, wireless services, and peer-to-peer data sharing on the Internet are not on the World Wide Web.

However, never let the facts confuse the issue, as Groucho Marx often said. Since everyone seems to think that the Internet and the Web are the same, and since it makes little difference from a business and legal point of view, we will also consider the Web and the Internet the same.

Everything in this book that applies to the Internet also applies to the World Wide Web. Throughout this book, I use the words Internet, Net, Web, and World Wide Web, as well as the term "online," interchangeably. You'll also notice that, except for the word "online," these terms are capitalized. I couldn't tell you why, but that's the conventional way it's done.

## Using the Internet

Just about every business in the United States uses the Internet. Although less than half of the small businesses in the U.S. have a Web site, 90% of these businesses have Internet access.

E-mail is the most used Internet business tool. Customers, clients, suppliers, almost everyone you do business with, have come to expect your business to have an e-mail address.

Faxing can be done over the Internet.

Online banking is available on the Internet. Nearly all banks let you access your bank accounts, download statements, and transfer money between accounts.

Internet e-business services provide any business functions you want to farm out: billing, product fulfillment, shipping, bookkeeping, customer records, payroll, taxes, legal, you name it.

Need a contract? Partnership papers? Buy-sell agreement? Legal documents and legal assistance are readily available on the Internet.

Large corporations are moving their purchasing online.

Nationwide phone and address directories and Yellow Pages are on the Internet. The Post Office lets you look up zip codes and calculate postal rates. You can buy postage over the Internet.

United Parcel Service (UPS), Federal Express (FedEx) and other shippers have Web sites to schedule and track packages. You can process all your shipping documents on the Internet.

If you are having problems with your computer or one of your software programs, almost every computer and software manufacturer has its own

Web site, offering technical support and problem-solving help. You can often download a "bug fix" or a free upgrade to a program.

Many popular software programs can be downloaded from the Internet for a thirty-day free trial. You no longer have to waste time and money on software that does not meet your needs. Web based software is covered in **Chapter 5: Web Based Computing**.

## Market Research

Businesses use the Internet for market research. You can study the Web sites of competing businesses, see what they are offering, see what they are charging, see the newest trends, pick up some ideas to use on your own Web site.

If you are researching a new product you want to carry, or a new type of business you want to start, or a franchise you might want to invest in, or a company you might want to buy from or sell to, the Internet can probably provide more background information than anywhere else.

The U.S. Census Department provides a wealth of free demographic and economic information about communities all over the U.S., collected from the 2000 Census. The Census is a marketer's dream come true.

## Legal, Tax, and General Business Research

A problem every business has struggled with over the years, is obtaining current and accurate tax and legal information: What government agencies are making what demands on your business? What IRS laws have recently changed? Where can you get government forms and instructions, and where do you send them?

The Internet makes these answers much easier to find. No more telephone calls to the wrong office, no more letters to government agencies that never get answered. Every federal agency has a Web site: the IRS, the Small Business Administration, the Patent and Trademark Office, The Copyright Office, The Department of Commerce, the Federal Trade Commission. These government Web sites include information about all the laws discussed in this book. Many government publications are online, and you can download many of the forms you need. A list of government Web addresses is included at the end of the book.

Many state government agencies have Web sites, with information about your state's employment laws, income tax laws, sales tax laws, consumer protection laws, and other regulations affecting businesses.

More and more government agencies are allowing businesses to apply for business licenses, get permits, and file tax returns on the Internet. Instead of standing in line for half an hour at City Hall to get an application, you may be able to do all of your paperwork on the Internet.

Some federal agencies, particularly the U.S. Patent and Trademark Office, are trying to get all applications and forms filed online. The Patent and Trademark people are going out of their way to make it faster and easier to file online—and to make it slower and more difficult to file with paper forms sent through the mail.

You can get legal and business advice, absolutely free, from the many business periodicals, legal publishers, business consultants, CPA firms, and law firms that put their magazines, newsletters, bulletins and updates on the Internet. Trade, professional, and small business organizations have Web sites where people discuss business, answer each other's questions, and share information. It's like a merchant's luncheon without going out to lunch, and you get to "talk" with people all over the country and the world.

Gathering information from the Internet requires caution and skepticism. There is a sea of snake oil out there. Anyone can post anything on the Internet, and they can do it anonymously or with a fraudulent name and phony credentials. People may be trying to sell you something, trying to disguise their advertisements as factual information or an editorial, or trying to impress you with information that may be incorrect or out of date. If you read something on the Internet, consider the source, verify it, and check other sources before relying on it.

# Chapter 3:
# Getting on the Internet

*"It's like 1908 in the automobile industry. Twenty years later, it was hard to find a horse in a major American city."*
**—Dick Brass, Microsoft Corporation**

There are several ways to access the Internet, depending on your budget and the available services in your area.

For most people, at this stage of technology development, Internet access requires a computer, a modem, a telephone line, and an Internet Service Provider (ISP). This system of getting on the Internet is called a "dial up" connection, referring to the process of your modem dialing your Internet Service Provider, which in turn hooks you up to the Internet.

A step up in speed—and cost—is an ISDN (Integrated Services Digital Network) connection. And a further step up is DSL (Digital Subscriber Line). These services are not available in all areas, and they may be more costly than your budget allows. Both require a connection through telephone wires.

Cable television companies offer Internet access on their cables, eliminating the need for a telephone line. Wireless and satellite Internet connections are also available.

With an Internet business, you will be spending a lot of time online, so I suggest you get the fastest and most reliable connection that meets your budget. The Internet can be slower than molasses in January if you don't have a good, fast connection.

## Computer and Modem

A fast, powerful computer will be a tremendous asset to navigate the Internet. Older computers will make Internet connections slower, more difficult, and much more frustrating, and in fact may not work at all on some of the more complex, interactive Web sites.

In addition to a fast computer, make sure you have a fast modem. A modem is an electronic gadget that hooks your computer up to your telephone line. Modems can be installed inside your computer, or can sit on your desk (and clutter it up even more). Modems are rated by speed, how fast they work making Internet connections. Modems are very inexpensive. Buy the fastest modem available. Get rid of your old modem if it is slower than the fastest modem on the market.

Get a hardware (hard) modem instead of a software (soft) modem. Hard modems have their own built-in computer chips (their own hardware), and are faster and more reliable than soft modems.

Local computer stores will install a modem for little or no extra cost.


## Telephone Line

Except for cable connections, wireless connections, and high speed DSL connections, the Internet is accessed through your regular telephone lines.

You can use the same telephone line as your home or business phone or your fax. But if someone tries to call or fax that line while you are on the Internet, they'll get a busy signal, or they may get a ringing phone, nobody picking it up, although new modem technology will soon allow you to be on the Internet and still get calls. For most phone lines, you cannot use call-waiting because it will disconnect your Internet connection. If you have voice mail, the voice mail will take messages while you are online. Some voice mail systems can flash a message on your computer while you are on the Internet, letting you know who called.

You will have to decide if you can share lines without disrupting your business: Are you willing to sacrifice incoming calls or incoming faxes while you are online? Or do you need to get another telephone line just for the Internet?


## Internet Service Provider (ISP)

For most people, connection to the Internet is through an Internet Service Provider, an ISP. You cannot go directly to the Internet from your computer. Your computer, using your modem, dials up your Internet

Service Provider, and the ISP connects you to the Internet. Your ISP sends and receives your e-mail (although e-mail is available from other Internet services as well; discussed below).

Don't confuse an ISP with a Web host. Your ISP connects you to the Internet. Your Web host puts your Web site on the Internet. Many ISPs also offer Web hosting services, but there is no need to use the same company for both services.

Millions of people use the giant national ISPs such as America Online (AOL) and EarthLink. But many other people use a regional or local ISP, often a small, locally-owned business, with maybe a few hundred or a thousand customers. The giant companies like AOL and the local ISPs offer the same basic services.

You want an ISP, whether is it local or national, that has a telephone number in your local area, one your modem can dial up without incurring long-distance charges. If you live in a city or large metropolitan area, this is not a problem. But if you live in a rural area, make sure the Internet provider has a local number. (The provider does not have to be located in your local telephone area, it only needs a modem call-up number in your area). The Internet can get mighty expensive if your modem places a long-distance call every time you go online. Some providers have an 800-toll-free call-up number for customers who are out of their local service area, but the ISPs charge higher fees for the toll-free Internet service.

The quality, ease, and speed of your connection to the Internet is also of prime importance when selecting an Internet Service Provider. Some ISPs are overloaded, often causing busy signals when you try to log on. Some ISPs have poor connections, disconnecting you from the Internet without warning (although this is often a problem with the telephone line, or with your modem, not the ISP). A local ISP may be much more reliable—or much worse—than a large ISP. Talk to other people who use local ISPs and get their feedback.

Technical support is another issue. You won't need technical support often, but when you do it's mighty nice not to be put on hold for ten minutes. And you shouldn't have to pay extra for it, either. Many Internet Service Providers offer a toll free number for tech support. Local ISPs usually have quicker and more friendly technical support than the large national companies.

You need software to access the Internet. ISPs provide the software you need at no additional cost. Some older computers cannot run the newest Internet software. If you have an older computer, talk to your Internet Service Provider before investing time and money in a service you cannot use.

Many ISPs offer a free trial period or guarantee you a refund if you don't like their service. You are not stuck with an ISP you don't like. You can cancel and try another company.

Some ISPs offer free access to the Internet. These providers make their money off advertising, which may or may not be intrusive or a nuisance to you. Free ISP connections tend to be slower and less reliable than ISPs that charge for their services. And every free ISP will put an ad for itself on every e-mail you send out.

Many businesses use more than one Internet Service Provider: a main, full service ISP, and a second ISP as a backup. If your main ISP goes down, or if you are away from your ISP service area, you can log onto the Internet using your backup ISP.

Every Internet Service Provider will require you to accept their terms and conditions. Read the agreement! ISPs often claim to offer unlimited Web access, but their definition of "unlimited" may not be the same as yours. Some ISPs restrict the amount of Net access time per month you are entitled to. Internet Service Providers often restrict or prohibit continuous usage, running a Web server, sending spam, setting up a site that generates too much traffic, carrying on an activity that may cause the ISP legal problems, and other activities that could affect the Internet Service Provider or its other customers.

# Chapter 4:
# E-Mail

*"The great thing about e-mail is it turns off the politeness gene, even for Midwesterners."*

**—Jeff Bezos, founder, Amazon.com**

Every person on the Internet has an e-mail (short for electronic mail) address. Using e-mail, you can send messages, documents, photos, drawings to anyone in the world, and they can correspond with you, at no cost. E-mail messages take anywhere from a few seconds to as much as an hour to arrive, depending on how busy the Internet is, and how dependable your Internet Service Provider is. Like regular mail, you must know a person's or company's e-mail address in order to send them e-mail.

All ISPs let you have an e-mail address as part of their regular service. Most ISPs allow you to have more than one e-mail address, at little or no extra charge.

You make up your own e-mail address, often your name or your business name, or an abbreviation, or a pseudonym, followed by @, followed by your ISP's identification. Usually, e-mail addresses are all lower case, because the Internet ignores capital letters. There are no spaces in e-mail addresses. If you put in a blank space between words or symbols, the e-mail will not be delivered. Some e-mail addresses use an underline mark to represent a space, such as "princess_julia@saber.net" which works fine, although it is a bit confusing for Internet novices.

Smaller ISPs with fewer customers have fewer names already claimed as e-mail addresses, which means you're more likely to be able to pick one you like. If you are the Acme Company and want your e-mail address to be your business name, you have a much better chance to get acme@local.net than acme@aol.com. America Online (AOL) probably gave out Acme—and every other business name—years ago. If you go with AOL or another of the national ISPs, or with one of the free services such as Yahoo or HotMail, you may be stuck with a number or a code as your e-mail address.

When you get an e-mail address through your ISP, you access your e-mail only through your Internet Service Provider. If you switch ISPs, you will not be able to keep the same e-mail address, although most ISPs will forward your e-mail to a new e-mail address for a certain period of time. Some charge a fee for this service.

If you have e-mail with a local ISP, when you are travelling away from home, you may find that you cannot get your e-mail from a locality not served by your ISP. This is not a problem if you have an e-mail account with a national ISP or with one of the many Internet-based services, such as Yahoo or HotMail, that offer free e-mail.

Most business people have more than one e-mail account. They use a free account as a junk mail collector: the e-mail address they give out whenever they have to register to gain access to someone's Web page. Another e-mail account can be used exclusively for private or business use, or when travelling.

If you want your business e-mail to look professional, be sure the service you use does not tack on an ad. Many of the free e-mail services put an advertisement on every e-mail sent. If all of your e-mails to your customers include a message like "Get your own free Hotmail account," that looks very unprofessional. Prospective customers will be wondering if this is a real business.

E-mail addresses must be precisely typed. Misspell a word, get a digit wrong, add or leave out a dash mark or an underline mark or a tilde ~ and the e-mail will never get delivered. If you have a long or strangely named e-mail address, more people are likely to mistype it and not reach you.

If you will be sending out a large volume of e-mail, contacting hundreds of customers, or publishing an e-mail newsletter, check with your ISP or Web-site host about restrictions on bulk e-mail. Some service providers do not have the capability to process large volumes of e-mail, other providers don't want the legal and public-relations problems sometimes associated with bulk e-mailings.

Web sites can be set up so visitors to the site can e-mail the owner of the site directly from the site. Your Web site can have e-mail addresses that include the name of the Web site, such as info@yourbusiness.com, catalog@yourbusiness.com, any-name-you-want@yourbusines.com. This is  covered in **Chapter 18: Web Site Design**.

## E-Mail Security

E-mail is not secure. You have no control over who will see an e-mail you send out. Any e-mail you send to someone can get forwarded to others, copied, printed out, and saved to be read again and again. E-mail, if not deleted, can linger in a computer's hard drive for years.

A snoop with technical skills can hack into your ISP and look at your e-mail while it is sitting on your ISP's server. If a hacker can break into your own computer, the hacker will have little trouble reading your e-mail. However, just because e-mail is not secure does not mean it will be seen by unauthorized individuals. How many people really want to hack into your ISP just to read your e-mail?

If you are sending and receiving confidential information, or if you will be getting credit card orders via e-mail, you should consider e-mail security measures. Talk to your ISP about security and privacy measures the ISP has in place to protect your e-mail from prying eyes.

Encryption software is available for e-mail. Encryption jumbles your messages into unreadable code. But the recipient of the encrypted e-mail must also have the software to unscramble the message.

## E-Mail and the Law

When you make a sales offer, or agree to a purchase, or make any other business commitment using e-mail, you have created a binding, legal contract, if the other party decides to hold you to it.

Think out your e-mail business dealings as carefully as you would a formal contract. Once an e-mail is sent, there's no retrieving it. As Stevie Wonder sang, it's "Signed, sealed and delivered...I'm yours." Consider holding the e-mail for a day before sending it, just to be sure you got everything the way you want it. Give it a fresh re-reading the next morning before sending it. Do not send anything by e-mail that demands security or might cause you a problem with privacy. Delete sensitive information as soon as possible.

The magic of e-mail is a double-edged sword. Because e-mail is informal by nature, people type things in e-mail that they'd never write in a letter, let alone say to someone's face. E-mail, being so spontaneous and often not well thought out, has gotten some people in legal hot water. Lawyers often talk about "smoking gun" documents in legal cases. E-mail has become the #1 source of damaging evidence in many legal disputes.

# Chapter 5:
# Web-Based Computing

*"If there's any dispute between you and the software provider, they can shut you down. They hold your business in their hands. They move to Number One on your list of creditors."*
**—Kathryn Morton, Avonlea Traditions**

The Internet has introduced the concept of Web-based computing (also known as "Internet Distributed Services" or IDS), where some or all of your software resides on the Internet instead of on your computer, and your data is stored on the Net instead of on your computer.

Your business data is accessible anywhere, anytime, from any computer with Internet access. You don't have to lug a laptop all over the world. You can share access to your company records with your accountant or business partners.

## Application Service Providers (ASPs)

Web-based computing services are available from companies that call themselves Application Service Providers (ASPs) or sometimes Internet Business Services (IBSs), Application Management Providers (AMPs), Business Service Providers (BSPs), or Full Service Providers (FSPs), different titles for the same thing: companies that rent you software and space on their servers to run and store your business ledgers, files and documents. The Application Service Provider is responsible for software upgrades, backups, and network security. Some people refer to this as "subscription computing:" you pay so-much per month to "subscribe" to software.

Web-based computing brings the risk of losing access to data, when the Internet can't be accessed or a server goes down. A slow Internet connection will be mighty frustrating if you need your numbers immediately.

Privacy issues will be a constant problem. The ASPs promise to keep your private information confidential. But they don't offer much more than their word as assurance—along with legal disclaimers that they may not be able to keep their word. And there is a small but definite risk of theft and security breaches on the Internet.

Most ASPs are new, and no telling how well they'll deliver on their promises, how long they'll stay in business, and how do you rescue your data if the ASP "heads south?" If you decide to use an ASP, pick one that is well-established and profitable. If the ASP is a publicly-owned company, you can obtain the ASP's annual financial statements to see if the business is struggling or doing well. This may seem far fetched, but several large, unprofitable ASPs have already folded, causing no end of problems for their abandoned clients.

Some ASPs offer software from well known software companies, a range of products that you may already be familiar with, that you can purchase on your own should you no longer want to rent the software from an ASP. Some ASPs, however, create their own software. You should determine how good and useful the software is, and how easy it will be to learn, before committing yourself to an ASP. And if you leave the ASP, can you purchase the software you've been using, or will you have to start all over with a different program?

Does the ASP offer a service guarantee? Does the ASP offer insurance or reimbursement if your data is lost and must be recreated?

Because of these real risks, it is not clear how popular Web-based computing will become, but it is likely to be used to some extent by many businesses. I personally would not use an ASP to store or process anything confidential, and I would have my own backup, just in case.

Read the ASPs contract. Don't be surprised if the ASP disclaims any liability for anything that might happen to data for any reason, including flaws in the ASPs own programs.

## Advantages of Application Service Providers:

1. You don't have to purchase software.
2. You don't have to worry about problems loading software or incompatibility with other software on your computer.
3. You don't have to deal with upgrades, they're automatic (but also see "Disadvantages" below).
4. You don't have to worry about your hard drive crashing and wiping out all your files.
5. You can access and work on your documents from any computer hooked up to the Internet.
6. You can share information with anyone who has Internet access.
7. You don't have to worry about losing your files if your computer is stolen or destroyed.

## Disadvantages of Application Service Providers:

1. A bad Internet connection will interrupt your work.
2. You must have an Internet connection that easily allows you to be connected for possibly hours at a time. If your modem shares a telephone line with a fax or voice phone, using an ASP will not be practical.
3. When the ASP upgrades the software, will you be happy with the upgrade? It is not uncommon to find that upgraded software has a serious bug that was not present in the older version. Upgraded software sometimes eliminates some of the functions found in the old version, possibly a function you rely on. Won't you love that?
4. If the ASP goes down, you will not be able to access your records until the ASP gets back online.
5. You risk security leaks, where unauthorized people gain access to your records.
6. If the ASP goes bankrupt, will you lose access to your files?

## Software From the Internet

One area of Web-based computing that is gaining widespread acceptance—and not dependent on Application Service Providers—is the acquisition of software from the Internet.

Many software manufacturers are offering their software through the Internet. You can download the software, and all upgrades, from the software manufacturer's Web site, automatically installed onto your hard drive, without need for CD-ROMs or floppy disks.

Downloaded software often comes with a thirty-day free trial period. You can download the complete software package and have unlimited use for thirty days. If you don't like it or can't figure it out, you don't buy it.

Trial versions of software do not require you to give out your credit card number until you are ready to buy the software. You are not in any way committed, and you do not have to worry about being charged for a product you decide you don't want.

If you do not buy the software, at the end of the trial period the software becomes inoperable. It is still sitting, dead, on your hard drive. You can usually access and retrieve your data, but you can no longer work with it. You can reactivate the software at a later date, if you choose to, by purchasing it. Or you can delete it from your hard drive.

If you do like the software and decide to buy it, only then do you give the software manufacturer your credit card number. Upgrades are usually included at no extra cost, usually for a year.

To find the software you want to try, log onto the manufacturer's Web site if you know it. Or use a search engine, entering the brand name or description of the software. Or look on the Web sites of the popular computing magazines; many of them have a "Downloads" page offering a variety of software to try out.

Just about every business has wasted money on some worthless boxed software that turned out to be too complicated to understand, or did not do the job. "Thirty-Day Free Trial" is one of the best things the Internet has to offer.

## Licensing Software

Technically speaking, when you purchase software, you are not legally buying it. If you read the fine print (instead of just blindly clicking "I Accept" like everybody else does), you will learn that you are "licensing" the software. This is the manufacturer's way of legally maintaining control of software misuse, such as unauthorized duplication or people stealing the codes to create other software.

Software manufacturers, not satisfied with licensing agreements, have gone even further to protect their rights. They have urged several states to pass a law called the Uniform Computer Information Transactions Act, UCITA for short. This onerous piece of legislation basically allows the software manufacturers to revoke your "license" to use their software if you violate the licensing agreement. If you violate the agreement, the manufacturers, under the UCITA law, can actually reach right into your hard drive and disable the software. Most likely you will never encounter UCITA or a software manufacturer breaking and entering your computer. If a piece of software vanishes from your computer, chances are it's just your computer being a computer (or your kid pushed the wrong buttons).

Just as you acquire licensing rights to software you "purchase," you can sell licensing rights to products or to content on your Web site, instead of selling the products outright. Licensing gives you the right to control the reproduction and distribution of your goods.

If you are offering a license instead of a sale, the information should be displayed prominently on your Web site. It should be stated simply, easy to understand. It should follow, as closely as possibly, industry norms. Read the licenses offered on other Web sites and use them as a guide to writing yours.

**"How is the Net transforming the company? It has the potential to be the company."**
—*Richard Keyser, President, W.W. Granger, nation's largest vendor of factory parts, Lake Forest, Illinois*

# Section Two:
# Starting an Internet Business

*"The transformation of business to e-business has a lot in common with white water rafting. The currents are strong and unpredictable, and there are dangerous surprises lurking beneath the surface. In spite of this, you can get where you want to go, you can remain in control, and you can have a lot of fun along the way."*

—Stuart Malin, Envisix Corporation

## Chapter 6:
# Starting An Internet Business

*"Though the statement 'Going online seemed like a cool thing to do' doesn't suggest a finely tuned strategic plan, that very rationale is behind a number of successful e-commerce sites."*
   **—Linda Formichelli, E-Commerce Business Magazine**

I imagine the majority of people reading this book have a good idea what kind of business they want to start, or they already have a working business.

If you are not already in business, there are a few important basics to consider. The Internet, by expanding your business beyond the local area, has added greatly to the opportunities you have. But the wrong business will fail on the Internet just as surely as it will fail in the real world. It's a business like any other, and it has to be run like one.

The well-known statistics often spouted by the Small Business Administration and other business organizations, that 60% of all new businesses fail the first year, is totally misleading. First of all, I think it is a flawed statistic. Nobody, not even the Internal Revenue Service, has been able to come up with a failure rate for businesses. They can't even determine how many businesses actually exist in the United States.

But even if the failure figures are accurate, just because 60% of new businesses fail, this does not mean your own business has a 60% chance of failure. There are some businesses, businesses that just weren't well thought out, that are virtually guaranteed to fail. There are some businesses, ones that were well thought out and planned, that have an almost 100% chance of success.

Your chance of success or failure has a lot to do with the kind of business you are starting, your ability to find and keep customers, your talent at running a business, and how well you prepare yourself for this new venture.

Starting an Internet business is a little like painting a house. A lot of the work is in the preparation. If prepared right, the job goes quickly and easily. If you take time to think out your ideas, to plan how you will proceed, and to learn how to run a business, you will have a much greater chance of success than someone who gives no thought to the process.

It is important to choose a business you'd enjoy operating and a business you are competent to operate. But people who choose a business solely on this criteria often fail, because they never researched the most important factor: the customers. You must force yourself, at least temporarily, to ignore your own interests and biases, and focus on the people you need to reach. You must do a little "market research," a fancy term for "look before you leap."

Are there people out there who want what you have to offer? Can you find those people? Can you convince them to buy from you, instead of from someone else who may be offering the same product or service—someone else who may be better known and who may have better prices?

Research is important, but more important, though, is to *just get started*. Getting into business is all about momentum. The Internet has opened up a world of opportunities, and customers, never before available to small businesses. You are no longer limited to a local area, with only local customers. You can create a Web site that makes your business look professional and prosperous. You can experiment with products, prices, and presentation. Unlike a local store, where you quickly get a reputation, good or bad, with a Web site you can start all over again every day, until you get it right. Figure out the best way to get started, and if necessary do midcourse corrections. You may not get it exactly right the first time, but just talking about it is not going to get you anywhere.

Every year, thousands of brand new companies get an office or a telephone line, hang out their shingle, and declare themselves open for business. The actual sequence of events doesn't seem to matter much. Entrepreneurs get into business every which way. And the first thing you have to do? As the gentleman on the carnival midway always says, Step Right Up.


## The "eBay Entrepreneur"

Even people who've never been on the Internet know about eBay, the first and the most successful of the online auction sites. Every day on eBay, and on several other auction sites, thousands of people bid on items offered for sale by thousands of other people. The auction sites charge a small fee to list an item, and take a small percentage of the sale price. Everything from old toys to new cars, from rare books to pinball machines, can be found on eBay.

Many of the people who are selling goods through the auction sites are actually operating businesses. Owners of antique and second hand stores use the auction sites to supplement their income. Flea market merchants have actually abandoned flea markets entirely, doing all their selling on the Internet.

Many "eBay entrepreneurs" got started selling a few things they dug out of the attic, sort of an online yard sale. They discovered they could make some money at it, and started finding more things to sell. Pretty soon these people had a dozen auctions going all at the same time, earning a steady income, devoting real hours to the venture.

What these "accidental entrepreneurs" may not realize is that at some point, their fun on the Internet has evolved from yard-sale income to business income.

The IRS says that anyone who is selling goods to make a profit, and doing so with a "reasonable degree of regularity" is operating a business. And anyone operating a business whose net profit (total sales less expenses) is $400 or more a year, must file a business tax return.

The "business" may be full time, part time, seasonal, home-based. It may have a business name, bank account, and all the local permits; or it may just be you, no business name, never filed anything, no one even knows it's there. It doesn't matter to the IRS. If you are earning money, you're in business for yourself. You are self-employed. And you owe taxes.

The "eBay entrepreneurs" are subject to the exact same laws that every business and every self-employed individual is subject to.

## Getting Started: What Do You Need to Do?

If you are already in business and moving to the Internet, you don't need to do anything, other than get on the Internet, of course. You already have the permits, licenses, tax identification numbers, bank accounts, bookkeeping, and all that fun stuff taken care of. There are no additional government requirements to start an Internet business.

You don't already have the permits? You're running a business and never got the paperwork and licenses and taxes taken care of? Don't panic, you are not alone. A surprisingly large number of new business owners just start, selling some product or offering some service, and never "set up" the business. But every one sooner or later has to do it. Either the bank, the local, state or federal government, or someone you do business with, will start making demands.

So if you haven't "TCB," taken care of business, now is the time to do it. It's kind of like going to the dentist. You know you have to do it. You know the longer you wait, the worse it will get. So just get it over with. It's not that hard. You don't even have to learn a new software program! Read on.

---

# Chapter 7:
# Legal Structure for your Internet Business

*"Our hobby time turned out to be our market study and research rolled into one."*
**—Mayra Donnell, founder, Mayari Handmade Soaps, Maine**

Every business, and every self employed individual, must have what's called a "legal structure," how the business is legally set up. If you don't make the choice yourself, the legal structure is chosen for you, by law.

There are four basic legal structures available to businesses: sole proprietorship, partnership, corporation, and limited liability company.

## Sole Proprietorship

A sole proprietorship is a one person business or a self employed individual who has not incorporated or set up a limited liability company.

The sole proprietorship is by far the easiest, least expensive, and most common form of business. Of the twenty-some million businesses and self-employed individuals in the United States, over 85% of them are sole proprietors.

Sole proprietorship is the "default mode" for an individual. As soon as you start your business, you are automatically a sole proprietor. You don't file a form or a registration to become a sole proprietor. It doesn't matter whether you've got your permits and licenses, or whether you filed a tax return. It doesn't matter what you call yourself or what you call your business. It doesn't matter whether you are working full time or part time. If you are earning some money, you are a sole proprietor.

There are many legal and tax issues sole proprietors need to learn about, but the two most important ones are (1) your legal liability, and (2) how you compute your profit for income taxes.

## Legal Liability of the Sole Proprietorship

Legally, a sole proprietor (the owner of the business) and the sole proprietorship (the business itself) are one and the same. All business debts and obligations are the personal responsibility of the owner of the business. Lawsuits brought against the business can be taken from the personal assets of the owner. Claims against the owner of the business, personal claims having nothing to do with the business, can be taken from business assets. In other words, a sole proprietor is fully and personally 100% liable for everything that happens to the business.

## Taxable Profit of the Sole Proprietorship

The sole proprietorship itself does not pay income taxes. The owner, the sole proprietor, pays personal income taxes and self employment (Social Security) taxes based on the profit from the business. The income from the business (sales, fees) less the deductible expenses equals the taxable profit.

The deductible expenses of your business do not include money you pay to yourself. You compute the business taxable profit before deducting any payments to yourself. This is a very important part of tax law that all sole proprietors must understand.

A sole proprietor is not an employee of his or her business. As a sole proprietor, you cannot put yourself on the payroll. You cannot pay yourself a wage and deduct it as a business expense. You can withdraw as much or as little money as you want from your business, but it is not a wage and it does not affect how much you pay in taxes. You pay tax on the profit from your business whether you withdraw the money from the business or not.

## Sole Proprietorship Tax Returns

Sole proprietors file a tax return, Schedule C (or in some cases Schedule C-EZ), which is part of the personal 1040 return. The profit or loss on Schedule C is combined with all of your other income on your 1040 to figure your taxes. Income taxes are covered in **Chapter 29: Taxes**.

Sole proprietors are also required to pay self-employment tax, which is Social Security tax. This tax is 15.3% of the profit from your business. (The tax you pay is actually less than 15.3% due to two deductions used in computing the tax). Self-employment tax is computed on Form 1040-SE and included with your 1040 tax return.

Self-employment tax can come as quite a surprise to new sole proprietors. You may owe little or no income tax but still owe a whopping amount to Social Security. All of the personal exemptions and deductions that reduce your income tax—married, dependents, special tax credits—do not apply to the self-employment tax.

## Partnership

A partnership is two or more people who start a business together but do not incorporate or set up a limited liability company. The laws that apply to sole proprietorships also apply to partnerships.

Like a sole proprietorship, a partnership is the "default" mode. If you do not set up another form of business, you and your partners are automatically in a partnership.

## Legal Liability of a Partnership

Like a sole proprietorship, you and your partners are personally liable for the debts and obligations of your partnership. A creditor of the partnership, or someone who has won a lawsuit against the partnership, can go after your personal assets.

Even more serious are the legal problems your partners can cause you. All of the legal obligations of the partnership are your personal obligations. If your partner borrowed money for the business, or signed a contract for the business, or got sued over the business, you are personally liable for those obligations, even if you had nothing to do with them, even if you didn't know about them. Creditors of the partnership, if they cannot get full pay from the business itself, can come after any and all partners. Creditors do not have choose which partner to go after. A creditor can sue you personally for 100% of the obligation.

A partnership is by far the riskiest form of business to start, just because someone other than yourself (your partner) can expose you to unlimited legal liability.

## Taxable Profit of the Partnership

Like the sole proprietorship, partners are not employees of their partnership. Money withdrawn from the business by the partners is not a wage, and is not a business expense.

The partnership itself does not pay income taxes. The profit or loss from the partnership is divided among the partners according to each partner's percentage of ownership. Each partner pays personal income tax on his or her share of the profits, which, like the sole proprietorship, are computed before any deduction for payments to partners.

Partners, like sole proprietors, must pay self-employment tax. Self-employment tax is explained above under **Sole Proprietorship Tax Returns**.

## Partnership Tax Returns

Partnerships file a tax return, Form 1065, but the partnership itself pays no income tax. All partners get a copy of Schedule K-1, reporting their taxable share of the partnership profits. Each partner pays personal income tax on his and her share of the profit, on Schedule E of the regular 1040 tax return. Each partner is taxed on his or her share of the profits whether distributed to the partners or not. Income taxes are covered in **Chapter 29: Taxes**. Each partner pays Self employment tax, the same as sole proprietors (see **Sole Proprietorship Tax Returns**).

## Husband and Wife Partnerships

When a husband and wife run a business together (a business that has not been incorporated or set up as a limited liability company) they have two options:

1.They can structure themselves as a partnership, legally sharing ownership of the business. Or,

2.They can choose one spouse to officially own the business as a sole proprietor. The spouse who is not the sole proprietor can either be on the payroll as an official employee; or can work in the business with no official designation, neither an owner nor an employee.

Each choice involves different tax returns, different taxes, different fringe benefit rules, and different Social Security taxes and benefits. It is an important issue that you should discuss with your accountant.

## General Partnership

The kind of partnership described above is known as a "general partnership." Most business partnerships are general partnerships. There are two other types of partnerships, "limited partnerships" and "limited liability partnerships," which are very different from general partnerships. These "limited" partnership structures are rarely used by small businesses.

## Corporations

A corporation is recognized by law as a "legal entity," which means the business is legally separate from its owners. The owner or owners of a corporation (many corporations are one-person businesses) are called stockholders. They own shares of stock in the company. Owners of small corporations usually own most or all of the stock in their company.

## Corporate Limited Liability

A major difference between corporations and sole proprietorships or partnerships is the liability protection for the owners (the stockholders) of the corporation. This corporate liability protection is known as "limited liability." It is very limited, and widely misunderstood.

Generally speaking, the owners of a corporation are not personally liable for the regular business debts the corporation. If your corporation is unable to pay its debts, the creditors usually cannot get their money from the stockholders' personal, non-business assets. Sole proprietors and partners, by comparison, are personally liable for all business debts and obligations.

Corporate limited liability, however, applies only to debts incurred in the normal course of business: money owed to suppliers and other business creditors.

Corporate limited liability will not shield an owner from a lawsuit brought against the corporation. If your corporation is being sued for wrongdoing, you will be sued as well, personally. It is a myth, and a dangerous one, that a corporation will protect owners of corporations from lawsuits.

The corporation's limited liability will not protect an owner who acts with gross negligence, or who commits fraud, misrepresentation, slander, or any other misdeeds.

Corporations are required by law to follow some very strict rules not required of other forms of business, such as appointing officers, holding Board of Director meetings, keeping minutes of meetings, keeping a minimum amount of money in the bank account, and other required procedures. If the owners of a corporation do not follow the state's corporation laws exactly, most courts will hold the owners of the corporation 100% personally liable for all corporate debts.

Corporate limited liability will protect an owner from the actions of other owners. If one of your co-owners acts with gross negligence, commits fraud, signs a contract that cannot be completed, or does anything else related to the business, you are not personally liable for your partner's actions. You can lose everything you have invested in the corporation, but creditors and courts cannot come after your personal assets.

Corporate limited liability, even as limited as it is, is not a sure thing. What the law says and what actually happens in the real world are not always the same. If business problems get to the lawsuit stage—which hopefully they never will, and in fact rarely do—you can never be sure where you stand legally.

## Corporate Owner-Employees

The owners of corporations are also employees of their corporations. Unlike sole proprietorships and partnerships, a corporation hires its owners as legal employees, on the payroll with regular payroll deductions. The corporation deducts the owner-employee's wage as a business expense.

## Corporate Taxes

There are two different types of corporations, with two different tax structures, regular corporations, and S corporations.

### Regular Corporations

A regular corporation, sometimes called a C corporation, pays corporate income taxes on its profits. But because the profits are reduced by wages paid to the owners, small corporations usually show little or no taxable profit: it's all paid out in salary.

Wages paid to the owners of a corporation are taxable to the owners, as regular employee wages. The owners have withholding taken out of their paychecks, and get a W-2 statement at year-end, just like getting paid from any other employer.

If the corporation does show any profit (after deducting all expenses including the employee-owner's wage), the corporation pays income tax on the profit. Then, what the corporation does with that profit can trigger even more taxes.

If the corporation retains the profit within the company, to use for business expenses, there is no additional income tax. But if the corporation distributes the profit to the owners of the corporation, it is called a dividend. A dividend is not a tax deductible business expense, so the corporation does not get a deduction for distributing dividends. But a dividend is taxable income to the recipient. The shareholder-owner of the corporation pays personal income tax on dividends received.

If you've waded through the tax-law confusion I've tried to explain, you may have figured out that corporate profit can be taxed twice: once as corporate profit, taxed to the corporation; and a second time as dividend income, taxed to the shareholders. This is what's widely known as "double taxation," the argument often used to scare people off of corporations.

It is a flawed argument. Most small corporations can easily (and legally) avoid double taxation, by raising the owner's pay to bring corporate profits down to zero. Within reasonable amounts, this is a legal tactic, but something you should get your accountant to help you with.

## S Corporations

The S corporation, also known as the Subchapter S Corporation (so called because it is covered in Subchapter S of the Internal Revenue Code), is very similar to the regular C corporation. S corporations have the same limited liability as regular C corporations. Owners of S corporations are employees of their corporations, the same a C corporations.

S corporations, however, do not pay income tax. S corporations are taxed like partnerships and sole proprietorships. Any profit is taxable to the owners of the corporation, not to the corporation itself. This is often called "pass through" taxation: the profits pass through the company untaxed.

However, unlike a partnership or sole proprietorship, owners of S corporations are also employees of their S corporations, just like owners of regular C corporations. S corporation owners pay income taxes on their wages.

An S corporation gets to deduct the owner's salary in determining its taxable profit. If the S corporation has any profit after paying wages, that profit is taxable to the owner. So an employee owner of an S corporation will pay taxes on wages earned working for his corporation, and will also pay tax on any corporate profits.

Don't confuse this with the double taxation of regular C corporations. S corporation profits are taxed only once. But some of the profits are taxed as wages, and some of the profits are taxed as corporate profit. The corporation's owners pay all the taxes.

There are several other differences between S corporations and C corporations, but the tax aspects are the most significant.

## Corporation Tax Returns

Regular C corporations file Form 1120 or 1120-A. S corporations file Form 1120-S. Shareholders in S corporations get a copy of Form K-1, reporting their taxable share of the corporate profits, if there are any profits after paying wages to the owners. Each S corporation shareholder pays personal income tax on his and her share of the profit, on Schedule E of the regular 1040 tax return. Income taxes are covered in **Chapter 29: Taxes**.

## Why Incorporate?

Most new small businesses do not have many reasons to incorporate. The paperwork, the filing fees, the extra tax returns, the many strict rules, make a corporation an expensive and time consuming form of business.

Reasons to incorporate:

1. The limited liability. If you will be owing a lot of money to your suppliers, the corporation can protect your personal assets if the company goes bankrupt.

2. Taxes. Once a company grows to a point where you are making a lot of money, and you are getting into higher tax brackets, a C corporation may (or may not) save you tax money.

3. Ownership. A corporation makes it easy to add owners (shareholders), and to pass ownership to family members.

4. Financing. Outside financing, particularly equity financing, often requires a corporate legal structure. Equity financing is covered in **Chapter 14: Financing**.

5. Partnerships incorporate to protect the partners from problems caused by other partners. In a partnership, all partners are fully liable for debts and liabilities caused by other partners. In a corporation, individual partners are not personally liable for the actions and misdeeds of other partners (usually).

6. For self-employed individuals who are working as independent contractors for other businesses, a corporation makes it very clear to the IRS that you are not an employee of the company hiring you. The other business is technically hiring your corporation, not you as an individual. This is really an unnecessary step, as the IRS does not require you to incorporate. But it is a guaranteed way around the employee-versus-independent-contractor disputes.

You can start out as a sole proprietorship or partnership, and incorporate at any future date that it becomes a more desirable alternative. Your accountant should be able to explain all of the pros and cons to you, and reevaluate them every year or whenever some major change occurs in your business.

## Limited Liability Company

A limited liability company (LLC) is a form of business that combines some of the most desirable features of corporations, sole proprietorships, and partnerships. Limited liability companies offer the exact same limited liability as corporations—with the same warnings.

Limited liability companies are taxed like partnerships and sole proprietorships. All profits are taxed directly to the owners, who are officially known as "members." Like sole proprietors and partners in partnerships, members of LLCs are not employees of their business, a major difference from corporations.

Limited liability companies are much easier to set up than corporations, with fewer rules, and often lower taxes.

In most states, one or more persons can set up an LLC. Massachusetts is the only state that requires a minimum of two people.

## LLC Tax Returns

The IRS does not have a special LLC tax return. Limited liability companies file the same tax return as a partnership, Form 1065. All LLC members (owners) get a copy of Schedule K-1, reporting their taxable share of the LLC profits. Each member pays personal income tax on his and her share of the profit, on Schedule E of the regular 1040 tax return. Each member pays self-employment tax, as described above under **Sole Proprietorship Tax Returns**.

## Comparing Taxes

To give you an example how the different legal structures are taxed, let's take the example of a single-owner business that makes a profit of $30,000, before paying any money to the owner of the business. For the corporation example, the owner pays himself/herself a $30,000 wage. Let's assume the owner has no other income, is single with no dependents, and takes the standard deduction. Here is how the federal taxes add up:

|                                                   | Income Tax | Social Security and Medicare | Total Tax |
| ------------------------------------------------- | ---------- | --------------------------- | --------- |
| Sole Proprietor                                   | $2,794     | $4,239                      | $7,033    |
| C Corporation                                     | $2,794     | $4,590                      | $7,384    |
| S Corporation                                     | $2,794     | $4,590                      | $7,384    |
| LLC                                               | $2,794     | $4,239                      | $7,033    |
| Partnership (husband & wife)                      | $2,494     | $4,239                      | $6,733    |
| Partnership (50/50, 2 partners, combined taxes)   | $1,418     | $4,239                      | $5,657    |

The Social Security/Medicare tax is higher for corporations because payroll taxes, employer and employee combined, are higher than the self-employment tax. Income tax on the 50/50 partnership is lower because the two partners each earned $15,000, putting them in a lower tax bracket. The husband-wife partnership benefit from a lower tax rate for married couples.

These figures greatly simplify the tax calculations. But the basic point is that, for most small businesses, corporations and LLCs will not lower your income taxes.

## State Laws

The tax laws described above for the different legal structures are federal tax laws. Many states have the same or very similar tax laws, but some states have quite different laws for their state income tax. Some states do not recognize S corporations, and tax them as regular corporations. Some states impose corporate taxes on limited liability companies. When considering your options, ask your accountant about state requirements.

## Chapter 8:
# Choosing an Internet Business Name

*"It has no meaning, at least not in any language we know of. It just sounded sort of Internet-ish."*
**—Bernard Schneider, President and CEO, Intira,
explaining the company's name**

Choosing a name for your business has always been one of the fun things people get to do when starting out. There have always been many important things to consider when choosing a business name, but the Internet has added a new and important consideration: can you use your business name as your domain name?

There may be a hundred businesses in the United States called Main Street Music, but there is only one business on the Internet called mainstreetmusic.com. So do you try to find similar domain names, maybe mainstreet.com, mainmusic.com, or mainstreetmusic.org or.net or the new .biz, and hope your customers will remember your domain name?

Many new businesses choose their business name based on what domain names are still available. The business owner finds a domain name he or she likes, and registers the domain name first, before naming the business.

Many businesses are creating names that are basically meaningless, just so they can get a domain name the same as the business. One company I read about named itself Imtx, because no one had a domain name imtx.com. Now the Imtx Corporation owns imtx.com. Whether anyone will figure out what the company or product does is another matter. Domain names are covered in **Chapter 16: Domain Names**.

In addition to domain name availability, there are many important issues to consider when choosing a name for your Internet business:

1. Local legal restrictions. No two local businesses may have the same business name. When you file for a DBA—"Doing Business As" permit (see **Chapter 10: Permits and Licenses**) you will not be issued the DBA if another business in your city or county already has that business

name. Even if you are only on the Internet, and won't be setting up a store in town or even selling to local customers, only one business in your local jurisdiction can legally have a given business name.

2. State legal restrictions. Corporations registered in your state have exclusive state-wide use of their business name.

3. National legal restrictions. Businesses with national registered trademarks can stop local businesses from using the same business name, particularly if the national business is offering the same products or services as you are offering. The bigger and more famous the national corporation, the more legal muscle they have to force you to stop using a business name the same as, or even similar to, their trademarked name. This is covered in **Chapter 34: Trademarks**.

4. Business names that are easy to remember, easy to pronounce, and easy to spell will help your customers to find you again and will help tremendously when customers want to recommend your business to their friends.

5. Business names can be very descriptive (Computer Cave, Pinball Resource) or vague (Facets, Natural Choice), can be cute (We Be Designin') or professional (Julia Kaye Designs). Don't be trapped by a name that may limit future growth or change. What happens when Main Street Design moves to State Street? Or when The Silver Jeweler switches to gold or diamonds?

6. If your business will be listed in the Yellow Pages or in business directories, there may be an advantage to being close to the of the beginning of the alphabet.

# Chapter 9:
# Business Bank Account

*"Use common sense. The Web doesn't change the dismal economics of nowhere businesses."*
            **—Timothy J. Mullaney, Business Week Magazine**

As soon as you start your Internet business, before you open your doors, go to the bank and open a separate business checking account. Keep your business finances and your personal finances separate. Nothing can be more confusing than mixing business with pleasure, financially.

Talk to your bank ahead of time and find out the requirements for a business checking account. Some banks impose larger service charges and require larger minimum deposits for business accounts.

## Tax & Legal Requirements for Bank Accounts

No federal law requires you to have a bank account. The IRS does not require you to deposit your income in a bank account. The IRS *does* require you to report all income, whether deposited in a bank account or not.

The states do impose rules on business bank accounts. Many states require you to have a DBA ("doing business as") certificate before you can open a bank account in your business name. DBAs are covered below.

Some states require all businesses to deposit all checks payable to the business, in a business bank account. In these states, cashing a business check is prohibited by law. So you may be required by your state law to have a bank account, if your business gets checks.

Although you should have a business bank account separate from your personal bank account, to make the paperwork easier, no law requires you to keep separate business and personal checking accounts (sole proprietors only; all other forms of business must have separate bank accounts). You can pay business bills from a personal checking account, and get a full business deduction. You can deposit business checks into a personal bank account, if your bank's rules don't prohibit such activity.

Most banks will require you to set up a business bank account before they will let you deposit or cash checks made out to a business name. If your business name is the same as your name (that is, you don't use a made-up business name), your bank will probably let you deposit or cash business checks without setting up a separate business account.

# Chapter 10:
# Permits and Licenses for Internet Businesses

*"We liken ourselves to that little windup toy that keeps hitting the wall until it finds a way around it."*
—**Ann King, co-owner, Blooming Cookies Catalog, Atlanta, Ga.**

All Internet businesses, and all self employed individuals on the Internet, are required to have federal, state, and local identification numbers, permits and licenses.

## Federal Identification

Your business will be required to identify itself on tax forms and licenses by either of two numbers: your Social Security number, or a Federal Employer Identification Number (an EIN). The identification number you use (your Social Security Number or an EIN) is also known as your Taxpayer Identification Number, or TIN.

If you are a sole proprietor, a Social Security number is the only identification you need unless you hire employees; or you are required to file an excise tax return (not required of most businesses); or you purchase or inherit an existing business; or your state or other government agency, a vendor, or your insurance company requires you to have an identification number. Then you must have the Federal Employer Identification Number.

Partnerships, corporations and LLCs must have the Federal Employer Identification Number whether they hire employees or not.

As you can see, although the federal identification number is called an "Employer" Identification Number, the EIN is used by any business that needs a federal ID number, whether the business has employees or not.

To get an Employer Identification Number, file Form SS-4 with the IRS. No fee is charged. The IRS can mail or fax the EIN to you. You can download a copy of Form SS-4 from the IRS Web site **www.irs.gov**.

## State Identification

Some states require their own business identification numbers, and some use the federal numbers. Contact your state's Secretary of State or Department of Business Affairs. Most state agencies have Web sites. Log onto **www.state.[your state's two letter abbreviation].us** to find out the state requirements.

## Federal Licenses

Most Internet businesses do not need any federal licenses. The federal government licenses businesses engaged in common-carrier transportation, radio and television station construction, manufacture of drugs, alcohol or tobacco products, preparation of meat products, manufacture or sale of firearms, and investment counseling. Information on federal licenses is available from the Federal Trade Commission, **www.ftc.gov**.

## State Licenses

States license many types of professionals, tradespeople, repair shops, and other service businesses. Some state licenses have minimum education and experience requirements, and insurance requirements. State licenses must be renewed every year or two.

Log onto your state's web site to learn about their licensing requirements: **www.state.[your state's two-letter abbreviation].us**.

## Local Business Licenses

A local business license, if required, is merely a permit to do business locally. Some localities require all businesses to get a business license. Some localities require licenses only for certain types or sizes of businesses. In some localities, no licenses are required at all.

Internet businesses have the same licensing requirements as all other businesses. Even if you are working out of your home, no storefront, don't hang out a sign, no one even knows you're there, you may be required to get a business license.

You can inquire at your city hall or county offices about licensing requirements. Business licenses always cost money and usually must be renewed every year.

## DBA (Doing Business As) Registration

When a business goes by any name other than the owner's real name, the business is being operated under what's called a "fictitious name," also known as an "assumed name" or, most commonly, a "DBA"—doing business as. Top Notch Computer Repair, Julia's Cafe, Bassic Music, are typical examples of fictitious names, DBAs.

People doing business under a fictitious name are required to file a Fictitious Name Statement (or Assumed Name Certificate, or DBA, or whatever it's called in your state) with the county where your business is located, or in some states, with the state's Secretary of State. States usually charge a fee to file a DBA, and require you to renew it periodically. Your state's web site probably has information about DBAs: **www.state.[your state's two-letter abbreviation].us**.

People doing business under their own real names, such as Samuel Thesham, C.P.A. or Samuel Thesham Design, usually don't have to register for a DBA. Partnerships, corporations and limited liability companies (LLCs) do not need DBAs unless they are doing business under a name other than the legal name of the business.

## Sales Tax Permit

Every state (except the few states that do not have a sales tax) issues sales tax permits, also called seller's permits, resale licenses, or something similar. Every Internet business that sells goods or taxable services must obtain a sales tax permit from the state where the business is located. The main purpose of a sales tax permit is to set you up to collect sales tax from your customers and remit the tax to the state.

Generally, sales tax is collected only from customers in your own state. Out of state sales are not subject to sales tax. You do not need a sales tax permit from any state other than your own, unless you have a physical location in another state. But the Internet, and state laws regarding Internet sales, has complicated the issue of what sales are and are not taxable. This is a complex and important matter for all Internet businesses. It is covered in **Chapter 29: Taxes**.

A sales tax permit, in addition to registering you as a seller, gives you the right to buy goods for resale without paying sales tax to your supplier. Goods that will be resold and goods that will be used in manufacturing can be purchased tax-free, using your sales tax permit.

You can find out about sales tax, and you may be able to download the forms to apply for a sales tax permit, by logging onto your state's Web site: **www.state.[your state's two-letter abbreviation].us**.

## Home Businesses

Home-based businesses are required to get the same licenses and permits as all other businesses. Home-based businesses are sometimes required to get additional permits not required of businesses in commercial locations. See **Section 8, Home Business**.

# Chapter 11:
# Insurance for Internet Businesses

*"Many companies are embarking upon a journey into cyberspace without fully comprehending the potential mischief that can await them."*
—**Harvey Pitt, Chairman, Securities and Exchange Commission**

Every business needs some insurance. Whether you are on the Internet or not, whether you are big or tiny, whether you have a separate business location or working from your home, you must be aware of insurance requirements and, just as important, insurance policy limitations.

Some insurance is required by law. Some insurance may be required by your landlord or by your bank if you get a loan. Some insurance is essential protection for your business and for you personally, as the business owner. And some insurance is optional: Do you want it? Can you afford it? Are the risks of not having insurance greater than the premiums?

Before covering insurance specific to Internet businesses, here is a brief rundown of common insurance needs of all businesses. This list covers the most important and most common insurance available to businesses, but the list is a small fraction of the many kinds of insurance you can spend your money on.

## Vehicle Insurance

Liability coverage on all business vehicles is mandatory in most states. If you use your personal vehicle for business, check with your insurance company to make sure you have coverage that includes business use. Insurance policies are very restrictive, and insurance companies are very unforgiving. If you have an insurance claim that involves business use, and if your policy does not specifically cover business use of your vehicle, the claim may be rejected outright by the insurance company. Business property inside a vehicle, such as merchandise you are delivering or equipment you are bringing to the office, is not usually covered by vehicle insurance.

## Fire and Extended Coverage Insurance

Fire and Extended Coverage insurance covers buildings and their contents—inventory, equipment, furniture, etc.—in case of fire, lightning, storms, explosions, smoke damage, riot, and damage caused by aircraft or vehicles. Extended coverage may vary from one insurance company to the next. Contents coverage may be restricted in dollar amount and what contents are actually covered.

Although your computer may be covered under a fire insurance policy, the data in your computer is usually excluded from coverage.

Extended coverage sometimes includes vandalism. Vandalism policies, which cover physical damage to your business premises, do not cover vandalism to your Web site, or vandalism to your computer files.

## Liability Insurance

Liability insurance pays for claims brought against your business because of bodily injury. A customer, or possibly a computer repair person visiting your business, slips and falls, breaks a leg and slaps you with a $50,000 lawsuit; it's not uncommon.

Liability insurance does not cover you, the owner, nor any of your employees. It does not cover injuries caused by vehicles or by defective products.

Liability insurance is mandatory in a few states, optional in others. But legally required or not, liability coverage is the most important to any business where customers, clients, delivery people, or people providing services to your business come to your door. One lawsuit by an injured customer can wipe you out: your business, and you personally.

## Products Liability

Products liability insurance covers products designed, manufactured or sold by the insured once the product leaves the business' hands. It covers the business in case the user of the product sues for injury or property damage. The courts generally hold manufacturers strictly liable for any injury caused by their product, sometimes even when the product has not been used correctly.

Distributors, wholesalers, and retail stores can sometimes be liable for products they sell, though not usually. If the products are in their original packages, and if the retailer provides no assembly or advice, the risk is greatly reduced. Some manufacturers will indemnify retailers against product liability claims (sometimes called a "vendors endorsement").

Products liability insurance covers products sold through your Web site. But the Web site itself—the words and illustrations—is not considered a "product" and not covered by product liability insurance.

## Malpractice

Also known as "errors and omissions" and "professional liability" insurance. Protects you from lawsuits and losses from professional, ah, "mistakes." Malpractice insurance is often expensive and hard to find. It is sometimes available from professional societies or trade associations.

Internet "malpractice," that is, a Web site that may result in someone suing you over the site's contents, is sometimes covered under malpractice policies, sometimes not.

## Theft Coverage

Covers burglary (theft from a closed business) and robbery (theft using force or threat of violence). The cost of theft insurance varies widely, depending on what you are insuring, your location, and the theft protection on your premises: alarms, bars on the windows, dead bolts, etc.

Theft insurance does not include lost data inside a stolen computer, nor does the insurance cover data "stolen" from your Web site by a malicious hacker.

## Business Interruption

If your business closes due to fire or other insurable cause, business interruption insurance will pay you approximately what you would have earned. You can also purchase "extra expense" insurance, which pays the extra cost of keeping a business operating (such as renting temporary quarters) after a fire or other building damage.

Business interruption insurance does not cover you if your Web site goes down. It does not pay for loss of income if your computer is infected with a virus, or crashes.

## Worker's Compensation Insurance

Worker's compensation insurance (also known as "worker's comp") provides disability and death benefits to employees injured or killed on the job. Worker's compensation insurance provides medical payments for employees who become ill due to workplace conditions.

Most (but not all) states require employers to carry worker's compensation insurance for all employees, even if the employees are occasional or part-time. The employer must pay for the insurance.

Although a few states do not require workers' comp insurance, the employer is still legally liable for injuries an employee incurs on the job.

You, the owner of the business, may or may not be subject to workers' compensation insurance, depending on your state's laws. In many states, sole proprietors, partners in partnerships, owner/employees of small corporations, and owners of Limited Liability Companies are exempt from workers' compensation insurance. Some states make it an option; you decide if you want workers' compensation insurance for yourself.

## Internet Insurance

Most business insurance policies exclude coverage for Internet related problems. Regular business insurance policies often cover the physical damage, destruction, or theft of a computer, but these policies do not cover lost data, the consequences of lost data, or any problems your computer causes for customers, suppliers or people browsing your Web site. Business interruption insurance does not cover you if your Web site goes down, and it does not pay for loss of income if your computer is infected with a virus, or crashes.

Internet businesses have liability and loss exposure other businesses do not have, and insurance is available (sometimes called a "Net Secure" policy) for many of the unique situations Internet businesses encounter.

Coverage may include reimbursement for computer mishaps, glitches, outages, systems failures, loss or theft or corruption of data, fraud, and breaches of security on the Net. Some policies protect you from liability, similar to malpractice insurance, should you accidently spread a virus or cause other damage or loss to people accessing your site or using your service, or if you are sued over privacy issues. Some policies cover loss of income due to Web-related mishaps, similar to business-interruption insurance.

None of the Internet insurance is required by law, and truth to tell, some of it is so expensive, and deductibles so high, that most Internet businesses just do without.

## Purchasing Insurance

Most insurance companies offer a Business Owner's Policy (a "BOP") or All Risk Insurance, combining many coverages in one policy, although Internet insurance is not included in any standard BOP or All Risk insurance package.

Insurance companies are competitive, offering different rates, packages and premium payment plans. Many insurance policies offer much lower premiums if you opt for large deductibles.

It is a good idea to shop around. Pick an agent or broker who works with businesses regularly and who has some familiarity with Internet businesses. Make sure you are dealing with a solvent, reliable insurance company, one with a good reputation for settling claims. Your agent can show you the company's rating, or check with your state's insurance department.

And finally: Read the policy carefully before you pay for it, not after you've suffered a loss you *thought* was covered.

### Insurance for Home-Based Business

Home businesses have special insurance needs and are subject to restrictions on some insurance policies. This is covered in **Section 8: Home Business**.

---

# Chapter 12:
# Franchise Businesses

*"Competition can develop overnight. It says a lot about barriers to entry on the Internet. That is, there aren't a whole lot of them."*
**—Steve Pelez, former CEO, RedLadder, bankrupt dot-com**

A franchise is an individually owned business operated as though it was part of a large chain. Midas Muffler, McDonalds, and H&R Block are examples of well known national franchises. Under a franchise, services and products are standardized. Trademarks, advertising and store appearance are uniform.

Most franchises work this way: The franchise corporation (the franchisor) sells you (the franchisee) the right to use the franchisor's name and sell the franchisor's products or services. Franchisees pay a sign-up fee to join the franchise, pay for the costs of setting up the business, and pay ongoing royalties or a percentage of sales to the franchisor. Many franchisors require franchisees to buy all inventory, equipment and supplies from the franchisor.

The franchisor provides franchisees with a business plan and many, many rules that you must follow. Some franchises are stricter than others, but one issue that every franchisee should be aware of is how the Internet fits into the business plan.

While there are as yet no national franchises that are Internet-based businesses, many franchise businesses will benefit from having Web sites. And Web sites can lead to unique problems for franchisees.

One of the biggest issues for franchisees is territorial rights, called "encroachment" in the franchise agreements. Franchisors offer franchisees exclusive rights to an area: only one or a limited number of franchisees in a town, or within so many miles or so many city blocks. With the growth of the Internet, encroachment becomes a much larger problem. What if another franchisee, or the franchisor itself, starts selling over the Internet, to customers within your exclusive area? This should be spelled out clearly in your franchise agreement.

In addition to the problem of encroachment, some franchisors restrict what franchisees can do on the Internet, even what domain names you can or cannot use. Some franchisors want total control over any Internet site that has the franchise name in it.

People buying into franchises, and people who already own franchises, must study their franchise agreements, to determine if Internet sites and Internet sales are allowed, prohibited, or otherwise restricted.

## Retail Mall Merchants

If you have a retail store in a mall—a real shopping mall, not an online mall—some mall leases prohibit or restrict online activities by the tenants. Mall owners often get a percentage of sales as part of a store's lease. I guess the mall owners are afraid that a store's Internet sales will reduce the store's mall sales, reducing the mall owner's cut.

Read your lease. If there is any prohibition on Internet sales (or any out-of-store sales), it will be specifically spelled out. If you do pay a percentage of your sales to your landlord, check the lease to see if the percentage applies only to mall sales or to Internet sales as well.

## Chapter 13:
# Bookkeeping for the Internet Business

*"The Web is a lot cheaper, so you lose less money."*
**—John Kricfalusi, founder, Spumco Graphics**

Every business needs to keep track of its income and expenses. And basically, that's all bookkeeping is: a system to record the money coming in and the money going out.

Your accounting system (your bookkeeping system—the terms are used interchangeably) can be as simple or as complex as you want. The only legal requirement for bookkeeping comes from the IRS. The Internal Revenue Code states simply that a business "must keep records to correctly figure your taxes." What kind of records you keep, how detailed the records are, whether you use a pencil or a software program, whether you do the bookkeeping yourself or hire someone, is all up to you.

If you don't know bookkeeping, it is essential (and I am sorry to use such a demanding word, but "essential" applies here) to learn what bookkeeping is, and how to set up and keep a set of ledgers. Even if you get a top-notch software program to do your accounting, even if you hire someone else to do your accounting, you must understand how the accounting system works and how to interpret the numbers.

A good bookkeeping system will provide you with information essential to the survival of your Internet business. Only with a good bookkeeping system, one you understand and use, will you be able to evaluate your business and make any needed changes and plans for the future.

The numbers tell you how well or how poorly your business is doing. The numbers tell you where your money is coming from and where it is being spent. The numbers are a business owner's best friend. They are a critical tool for analysis and planning. And the numbers have a beautiful coldness about them. They don't lie.

But never suppose for a moment that an accounting system, no matter how sophisticated, will keep you out of financial trouble. Accounting information only records what happened in the past. It's up to you to use the numbers to learn from the past, learn from your mistakes, and to steer your business into successful waters.

If you are not familiar with the basics of bookkeeping, my book **Small Time Operator: How to Start Your Own Business, Keep Your Books, Pay Your Taxes and Stay Out of Trouble** (Bell Springs Publishing, 800-515-8050) includes a lengthy section explaining every aspect of bookkeeping.

But if I can't talk you into buying another book, here is an abbreviated version of Bookkeeping 101.

## Bookkeeping Basics, Part One: Income

Your income is recorded in three different records. If you post your books by hand, each of the three steps must be repeated, information recopied. If you have a good accounting software program, the steps are often combined. You enter the information once, and the software does the rest. But to understand how bookkeeping works, you should think of it as three separate operations.

Step 1. The first record is the bill (the invoice, cash receipt, or whatever else you want to call it) you give your customer. This can be a custom-designed invoice, a preprinted cash receipt out of a receipt book, a cash register receipt, or any other form that suits your needs and your business image. You should keep a copy of each invoice for your own records.

Step 2. The second record is your income ledger. You post all of your invoices to the income ledger. You can post each invoice individually to the income ledger, or you can batch the invoices daily or weekly and post summary totals to the ledger.

On income tax returns, the IRS asks for one figure: total sales. So for preparing income taxes, your income ledger only needs your total sales for the year. On sales tax returns, however, your state will require you to show taxable and non-taxable sales separately, and show the sales tax collected. So your income ledger should have separate columns to make it easy to fill out the sales tax return.

Beyond the income tax and sales tax requirements, your income ledger can be as simple or as detailed as you want. If you want to have different totals for different types of sales or different products, you can add a column for each category of income you want.

Step 3. The third income record is your bank account balance. When you deposit your income, you need to post the deposit to your bank records. Your bank account and your income ledgers are separate records, with different purposes. Although there are ledger systems that combine your bank account and your income ledger, you must be careful to view them, and to understand them, as two different ledgers.

## Bookkeeping Basics, Part Two: Expenses

Recording expenses is also a three-step procedure:
Step 1. When you pay a bill, mark "paid" on it, the date, method of payment, and the check number if you paid by check. And keep the original bill in your files. It is your most important proof if a vendor says you never paid your bill, or if the IRS questions your expenses in an audit.

If your business is a sole proprietorship, how you pay a bill is immaterial. You can pay by business or personal check, by business credit card or personal credit card. by money order, or by cash. The IRS allows business deductions no matter how they are paid.

If your business is a partnership, corporation, or limited liability company, you must be much more careful how the bills are paid. The business is legally separate from you, the owner, and the bills should be paid from business funds: business bank account, business credit card, business cash.

Step 2. If you paid by check, post the payment to your bank account record. If you didn't pay by check, skip this step.

Step 3. Every bill you pay must be posted to an expenditure ledger. The expenditure ledger has columns for the date, the payee, the check number (or payment method if not paid by check), and the total amount of the payment. The ledger also has different columns for different categories of expense, such as inventory, supplies, rent, etc. The most important function of the expenditure ledger is to separate different types of expenditures. You want to know where you are spending your money, and so does the IRS. For this reason, you cannot summarize a number of transactions on one line as you can with sales in the income ledger.

There are literally hundreds of different categories of expenditure on which small businesses spend their money. But you certainly don't want to post a ledger with a hundred columns, or even twenty columns. You need to pick the most important categories for your business, the high dollar categories, and the categories listed on your income tax return, and give the these categories of expense their own columns. Less important categories of expense can be combined.

## Bookkeeping Basics, Part Three: The Rest of the Stuff

The income and expenditure ledgers, along with the bank records, are the core records for all businesses. Additional ledgers, sometimes called subsidiary ledgers, may be needed for inventory control, accounts receivable (customers who owe you money), payroll, partnership records, equipment ledgers, job cost records: whatever records you need to keep track of your business and prepare your tax returns.

Whatever bookkeeping system you set up, here is the *real* secret recipe for success: Keep current. Post your books regularly. Get on a regular schedule, and keep to it. File the papers where you can find them. Don't let the paperwork pile up. Bookkeeping is enough of a nuisance when it is organized. If you start falling behind, getting the paperwork mixed up, lost invoices, boy, you're just gonna *love* bookkeeping.

---

# Chapter 14:
# Financing

*"If you have a credit card, you can create a business in about two hours. Buy a dot-com name, locate it on a server, contact a wholesaler. You can go from nothing to operational in two hours. The Internet probably increased the number of self-employed people in America by 25%. It could be 50%. We can't track it."*

**—Jerome Katz, St. Louis University**

Some hip philosopher once said, to a student who was very worried about something, "Don't sweat the small stuff." Then the philosopher paused and smugly added, "It's all small stuff." I always hated that comment, but it stuck with me. And, when it comes to financing an Internet business, in some ways, it too is the "small stuff."

I don't mean to downplay the need to be adequately financed when starting a business. But I do want to point out, before discussing the money—where it is, and where it isn't—that most people who want to start an Internet business have found a way to do it, with or without money.

## Start Up Costs

Before you try to figure out where the money is coming from, you must figure out what it is going to cost you to set up your Internet business. How much *does* it cost to start an Internet business? That's a little like asking how much it costs to buy a used car. So much depends on the type of business you are starting, and how luxurious or how thrift-store-cheap the business needs to be.

I'd suggest you start by making a list of all of your start-up costs. Here are some to consider:

1. Inventory. Inventory means goods for sale. If you are offering a service, you have no inventory. That cost is zero. If you are selling a product, will it be something you create yourself, something you manufacture, or something you buy to resell? How much initial stock-on-hand will you need? Can you make or purchase a very small quantity? Don't fall into the trap of ordering a large quantity of goods because you get a better price break. Buy the smallest quantity you can get, so if the goods do not sell, you won't be stuck with a garage full of unsalable inventory.

2. Business location. Do you need corporate offices with bamboo plants in the lobby? Do you just need a desk in the corner of your bedroom? Or something in between? If you will be working out of your home, location set-up costs are negligible. If you will be renting a separate business space, up-front costs will include rent and rent deposits, hook-up charges and deposits for utilities and telephone, and decorating or fix-up costs to get the business premises the way you want it to look.

3. Insurance. If you rent a separate business space, your landlord will most likely require you to have liability insurance and insurance on the building. Minimum coverage costs about $300 a year. If you work from home, you may need extra home insurance coverage. Minimum home-business coverage costs less than $50 a year.

4. Computer. If you already have a computer that can easily access the Internet, initial cost is zero.

5. Office furniture and equipment. If you are on a low budget, you can easily find the furniture you need for little or no money: desk, chair, file cabinet, shelving. You don't need much, and every second-hand store is full of old (and sometimes beautiful) office furniture at bargain-basement prices.

6. Office equipment. You'll need a phone, probably a multi-line phone, a fax machine, an adding machine, and a telephone answering machine (unless you have voice mail). You don't need much, but you do want to purchase quality, reliable equipment.

7. Office supplies. You may already have basic supplies like pens and paper, stapler, Scotch tape, etc. You may need to invest in stationery, business cards, brochures, and other promotional supplies.

8. Internet connection. You probably already have an Internet Service Provider, but you'll also need a Web site host. Web hosting costs anywhere from nothing (for a free Web site) up to maybe $50 a month for a comprehensive site package. There are many options, and prices, to choose from.

9. Banking and credit card processing. If you have to set up a new bank account, and if you have to set up a credit card merchant account so you can accept credit cards, the start-up costs can vary greatly, depending on which bank and which credit card processor you work with. You can spend anywhere from negligible amounts to several hundred dollars.

10. Web site design. If you hire someone to design your Web site, you can expect to spend anywhere from two or three hundred dollars on up to several thousand dollars, depending on the extent of the job, and on the fees the Web designer charges. There are many inexpensive, yet excellent Web designers looking for work.

11. Permits and licenses. You may need a local business license, a sales tax deposit, a "doing business as" permit, or some other legal document from your city, county or state. Costs typically are under $100 for all of them.

12. There is no #12, we're done. But I could list a hundred or more possible start-up expenses; and your particular business may have to lay out money for something or other you didn't plan on.

As you can see, some Internet businesses—those with expensive inventory and rented office space—might require thousands of dollars to get started. Some Internet businesses—home-based operations providing services or stocking very little inventory—can get started for next to nothing.

## Where's The Money?

Part of the reason for showing you how inexpensively an Internet business can be started is because this chapter may come as a great disappointment to anyone who has never started a business (and will come as no surprise to anyone who has).

There are three typical financing arrangements for businesses: (1) Self-financing: you put up your own money. (2) Debt financing: you borrow money. (3) Equity financing: you take on a partner or a stockholder, an individual who acquires an ownership interest in your business in exchange for start-up money.

## Self Financing

Just about every new business is at least partly self-financed, and many are 100% self-financed. A lot of new business owners cannot find anyone to loan them money or to invest in their untested and obviously risky ventures. Many new business owners self finance simply because they do not *want* outside financing and the risk and pressure of having to pay off a loan, and do not want to worry about, or share the profits with, a partner or co-owner.

## Debt Financing (Loans)

Bank loans to new small businesses are almost non-existent. Banks and other commercial lenders do not want to take a chance on new and untested businesses being started by new and untested entrepreneurs. Banks do make small business loans, but mostly to people who already have a business background, and people who have a sound business idea.

If you already have a business relationship with a bank, if you know the banker, if you are known and respected in the community, you chance of getting a loan from that bank are greatly increased. As in so much else in business—and life—it's not just what you know, it's who you know. (And it's collateral: a bank will want a mortgage on your home or on equipment or something of value they can grab if you can't repay the loan).

The U.S. Small Business Administration has several loan programs, but like banks, the SBA gives most of its loans to already successful businesses. The SBA does have a few micro-loan programs for new businesses. All SBA loan programs are on their Web site **www.sba.gov**.

Most loans to new businesses do not come from banks or the Small Business Administration. Most new business loans come from relatives, friends, and acquaintances. People who know you are much more likely to help finance your venture than an extra-cautious, policy-laden bank or government agency. Quite often, someone you know or someone you can be introduced to has some extra money, and might be willing to take a chance on your business if they like you and your idea and the terms of the financing.

When someone lends you money, you promise to pay it back, usually with interest. Most business loans are also personal loans: you, the owner of the business, personally guarantee the loan, and you must repay the loan whether your business succeeds or not, out of your personal non-business assets if necessary.

## Credit Card Financing

I give this form of financing its own little spot, because so many people launch their new businesses with their credit cards. You don't have to fill out loan applications, create business plans, make presentations, or convince anyone to give you money. You just run up the bills on the credit cards, and pay them off when you can—at astronomical interest rates. Go for it if you have to, but as soon as your business is showing signs of success, talk to your banker again. Bank loans are much less expensive than credit card financing.

If you are paying business expenses with a credit card, get a credit card just for business, and a different credit card for non-business purchases. Like having two separate bank accounts, having two credit cards will help you keep track of your business records much more easily. (I know, this sound like some bookkeeping class, not the real world. You'll probably be maxing out *all* of your credit cards to pay the business expenses.)

## Equity Financing

"Equity" means ownership. Equity financing usually involves an investor who buys into your business, as a partner in a partnership with you, as a shareholder who owns part of the stock in your corporation, or as an investor-member in your Limited Liability Company. Basically, you've acquired a partner, partner. The investor is taking a risk on your business, just as you are.

The best-known investors, the ones who get all the news coverage, are venture capitalists—individuals and firms that invest money in start-up businesses. But these big-money capitalists are rarely interested in most small businesses, Internet-related or not. Venture capitalists hand pick businesses that are at the cutting edge of technology, that are structured for fast growth, and that can make the venture capitalist, and not necessarily the business founder, a lot of money. Even in the best of economic times, only about 5,000 businesses a year get venture capital funding.

The typical investor, like the typical lender, is usually a friend, acquaintance or relative. Unlike a lender, however, the investor gets his or her money back only if the business succeeds. The owner of the business is usually not obligated to repay the investor out of personal non-business funds.

**Now What?**

Don't be afraid to explore your options. Talk up your business ideas with friends who may want to be involved. You will get yourself a fast education about business financing, and about how others perceive your business idea—and your own ability to pull it off. And remember what I wrote at the beginning of this chapter: Most people who want to start an Internet business have found a way to do it, with or without money. It's the truth. Don't sweat the small stuff.

---

# Chapter 15:
# Professional Help

*"Lawyers tell you everything is problematic."*
**—Soon-Chart Yu, Founder, Gazoontite Corp., San Francisco**

For new Internet businesses, the government requirements, the forms you must fill out, and the bookkeeping ledgers are easy enough for anyone to handle without the help of an accountant or an attorney. But some types of legal structures will need an accountant's help. Incomes taxes can get very complex. And occasionally, businesses will need help with contracts.

Most Internet businesses hire a tax accountant, usually an independent sole practitioner. The accountant prepares the business tax returns and occasionally consults with the business on specific issues as they come up.

I suggest you find an accountant who has several years' experience working with small businesses and independent professionals. The accountant should have a working knowledge of the Internet and the tax issues affecting Internet businesses. The accountant does not have to be a C.P.A. (a Certified Public Accountant), but the accountant should be a full-time professional with a lot of business clients.

The best way to locate a good tax accountant is to get recommendations from other business owners. Talk with the accountant, make sure you feel comfortable working with the individual. Choose an accountant who makes sense to you, an accountant who is able to explain laws and taxes so you can understand them. The best accountant in the world is worthless to you, if you can't understand what he's trying to explain. Remember, this is your business, not the accountant's. The final decisions are entirely up to you.

If you need help with your bookkeeping, some accountants help set up and explain bookkeeping. But you may do better to hire a bookkeeper, someone who does bookkeeping for a living. Bookkeepers are usually much less expensive than accountants. Bookkeepers may not be tax experts, but they know bookkeeping well. Again, get recommendations from other businesses.

Most businesses will not need an attorney for day-to-day business needs. You may need an attorney to help you set up a corporation, or draft a contract, or file a patent, or arrange a complex purchase or sale. Your accountant can most likely help you with all of these issues. Your accountant can also probably recommend an attorney to you if you need one.

**"When you are faced with a decision, make that decision as wisely as possible, then forget it. The moment of absolute certainty never arrives."**

—*Barbara Brabec, author, "Homemade Money"*

# Section Three:
# Web Sites

*"A smart business builds technology from the customer on back."*
—Management consultant Peter Keen

# Chapter 16:
# Domain Names

*"If you click past the famous brand names, you'll find tens of thousands of small businesses you never heard of, quietly making a go of it online, providing welcome relief from the big brands. The small businesses thrive because they're focused on narrow niches they know really well, allowing them to provide intensely personal service."*
—**Robert D. Hof, Business Week Magazine**

You can have your own Web address, called a "domain name," also known as a URL (Uniform Resource Locator), something like www.freebeer.com. This Web address is 100% yours, and stays with you as long as you pay the registration fees.

To get your own Web address, first you must pick a domain name that no one else has claim to. Many businesses want to use their business name, or a product name, or a product category, or some other name that is easily identified with the business. But with 32 million Web sites already on the Internet, this could be a difficult task. You may have to get very creative to come up with a domain name no one else has thought of. You must also be careful that your domain name is not trademarked or otherwise owned by another company (more on this below).

Web site names start with "www" which stands for the World Wide Web, followed by a dot (a period). Then the name you've chosen for your domain name, sometimes called a "second level domain" (the "freebeer" in www.freebeer.com) followed by a dot. Then a suffix, officially known as the "Top Level Domain" or TLD.

The best known and most used TLD is "com," short for commercial. The com TLD, or .com as most people think of it, is so pervasive today that the term "dot-com" has become synonymous with Internet businesses.

But there are other TLD suffixes you can use instead of com. The TLD suffix ".net" (short for network) and ".org" (short for organization) are available to anyone. Contrary to what many people think, .net and .org are not restricted to certain types of Web sites.

If a domain name you'd like to own, such as www.freebeer.com, is taken, you can try www.freebeer.net or www.freebeer.org. These are three different domain names, and all three endings—com, net, and org—are available to anyone on a first-come first-served basis. However, remember that most people automatically type a ".com" after every Web address. People may have a trouble remembering that your site ends in .net or .org.

In ads and promotions, many businesses don't include the "www" part of their domain name. Amazon.com is really www.amazon.com. For many Web sites you don't need to type in the www to get to the site. For example, typing either craftmarketer.com or www.craftmarketer.com will get you to the Craft Marketer Web site (a great site, by the way, for craft business books and information).

## New TLD Suffixes

In addition to .com, .org and .net, seven new TLDs are being added in 2001, greatly increasing your chances of getting a domain name you want, but greatly increasing the likelihood that people will have an even more difficult time remembering which suffix to type in.

The new TLD suffixes are broken into seven categories, restricting their use to certain types of Web sites. How the companies that assign domain names plan to screen applicants, police the use of restricted TLDs, or enforce compliance, remains to be seen. My guess is that, just as they gave up trying to restrict .org and .net, use of the new TLDs will be self-regulating. In other words, a free-for-all. The seven new TLDs are:

**.biz** Will be available to any business.

**.pro** Limited to professionals. Lawyers, certified public accountants, and physicians are, as of this writing, the only professionals "officially" authorized to use the .pro TLD. But domain name registrars may expand the definition of professional. Today, just about every self-employed individual calls himself a professional.

**.name** Unrestricted. Meant for individuals, for personal Web sites, but also available to businesses.

**.info** Unrestricted. Meant for sites offering information, however you would like to define "information." But again, available to any business.

**.coop** For cooperatives, although like .pro, it is unclear who will and will not be allowed to use this TLD.

**.museum** Meant for genuine museums, but I imagine businesses will find a way to make use of this suffix. Many businesses have some sort of display or mini-museum of the history of the products they sell. Whether this technically qualifies a business to use the .museum TLD, and whether it really matters whether the businesses qualify or not, is not yet known.

**.aero** Restricted to aerospace, airlines, air travel businesses.

## Alternative Domain Name System

There is an entirely different network of domain suffixes, and maverick businesses using those suffixes, totally unknown to most people. These wildcat TLDs (called "alternative root systems") include the suffixes .inc and .shop. The TLDs are not sanctioned by ICANN, the agency responsible for overseeing domain names. The TLDs are not found on search engine searches and cannot be accessed by many computers. But some of the largest national Internet Service Providers, and a growing number of smaller ISPs, are reconfiguring their servers to make the "hidden" TLDs accessible to their customers. The company that registers the unsanctioned TLDs, **www.new.net**, claims that 44 million Web surfers have access to their domains.

## Rules of Web Syntax

Domain names must obey the peculiar rules of Web language. The Web allows a domain name to have up to 64 characters, plus the TLD. The domain name cannot include spaces or ampersands (&).

So, for example, when the bookstore chain Barnes & Noble set up a Web site, it became barnesandnoble.com. You can glue two or three words together, as Barnes & Noble did, and have the awkward but possibly unique www.smithaddingmachinerepair.com.

You can have dashes, dots, or underlined spaces in your domain name. A domain name with a dash or a dot or an underlined space is a completely different domain than the same domain name with no punctuation. For example, "pinballrepair.com" is a different Web site than "pinball-repair.com" or pinball_repair.com" or "pinball.repair.com."

Another possibility is "ePinball.com" or "e-pinball.com" since people are already familiar with the "e" in front of site names. Any letter in front of your name will work, if people can remember it.

You can make up totally meaningless names out of real words or made up words. But cute spelling gimmicks—such as "KuteeKlothes"— can backfire, when no one, even your regular customers, can remember how to spell your name.

You can capitalize letters anywhere in a domain name. Capital versus lower case letters do not matter on the Web. The domain name www.yourbusiness.com is the same domain as www.yourBusiness.com, and www.YourBusiness.com. Using capital letters will help your customers correctly spell a long multi-word domain name.

If you choose a domain name with a suffix other than .com, you may want to see what business owns the .com domain name. If the .com site is offensive, or if it is a competing business, this may cause you problems, when your customers accidently type in .com, forgetting that your site ends in .org or .net or one of the new suffixes.

Finally, keep in mind that the Internet is global. You probably don't want your site name to mean "idiot" or "free sex" in Dutch.

## Checking Availability of Domain Names

Once you have a few ideas for your site's name, log onto any domain registrar's site (such as **www.NetworkSolutions.com**, the first and largest of the domain name registrars); or log onto any "who-is" site (more on "who-is" below); or log onto **www.icann.org**, the site of the agency responsible for overseeing all domain name registrations in the United States. Most of these sites maintain databases of all domain names currently registered. You can do your domain name research at any of these Web sites at no cost. Type in the domain name you would like, and you will get an answer whether the name is available or not.

If your domain name is available, you can immediately acquire rights to the domain name. Any domain registrar licensed by ICANN (listed on **www.icann.org**) will accept your application. You fill out an application form on the Internet and pay with a credit card. The domain name will be yours effective immediately. Initial registration can be anywhere from one to ten years.

Fees to acquire domain names vary, often dramatically, from registrar to registrar, as much as $35 a year for unclaimed .com names, less for .net and .org suffixes, much higher for other suffixes and for previously-claimed names being resold.

If you are not immediately ready to design your Web site, part of the domain registration fee usually includes, if you want it, a "Site Under Construction" or "Future Home of Your-Name-Here" notice when someone logs onto your site. Some registrars even offer the ability to create a small site (sometimes called a "business card") right on the spot. You simply type in what you want on your site, and it appears immediately. You can leave that rudimentary site up as long as you want.

If you cannot find an available domain name you like, you may be able to purchase a domain name from the person who already has the rights to that name. There are many choice .com names available from resellers, though expect to pay a lot more than $35 for this privilege.

Network Solutions and the other domain registration sites have a "classified ad" for-sale list of domain names. Or you can contact the domain name holder directly. Log onto the domain to see if there is a way to contact the site's owner. If not, there are several sites on the Web called "who-is" sites. You go to the "who-is" site, type in the domain name you want to know about, and the "who-is" site will tell you who owns the domain name and how to reach the owner. Domain name ownership is public information, made available to anyone who wants to search for it. There is no charge for a "who-is" search. To do a "who-is" search, try **www.whois.net**, or type in "whois" in a search engine.

You can also check back with Network Solutions or the other domain name registrars every few weeks to see if the site owner failed to renew the registration, making the site name up for grabs again.

## International Web Addresses

If all of your choices for a domain name are taken, you might consider an international Web address. In countries other than the United States, the suffix for Web sites is not .com or .org or .net. The suffix is two letters, referring to the country of origin; for example, ".au" for Australia, ".cn" for China.

Many countries restrict their Web suffixes to Web sites located within their borders. But over 80 countries around the world, including some tiny and obscure countries with names that sound like they come right out of an old Marx Brothers movie, have gotten into the easy-money act of licensing their domain names to any Web site, anywhere in the world, willing to pay their fee.

So if you cannot get www.pinballrepair.com or .org or .net you may be able to get www.pinballrepair.to (which is the suffix for the country of Tonga) or some other country's two letters. But again, keep in mind that most people automatically type a ".com" after every Web address. They may forget that your site ends in some two-letter suffix.

You register international domain names at the same place you register U.S. domain names, but be warned that international site registration is a lot more expensive than U.S. site registration. The foreign countries are selling these domain names at a handsome profit.

## Domain Renewals

You can renew your domain name as many times as you want. As long as you renew the domain before the current registration expires, you retain rights to the domain name indefinitely.

The company that handled your registration is supposed to notify you when your domain name renewal is due. But do not rely on being notified.

Know when your domain name is up for renewal, and renew the name well before the deadline. If you fail to renew your domain name, because you forgot, because you were not notified, because of any reason, the domain is shut down and the name is up for grabs.

Some domain name registrars offer automatic renewals, and Internet services offer reminders. These are helpful, but again don't rely on them. Losing your domain name will be a first-class disaster. The responsibility is yours.

## Multiple Sites / Multiple Businesses

Many businesses set up separate Web sites for different products or different areas of interest. Specialized and niche sites often draw more viewers than general sites. Web surfers often have trouble focusing when they visit a Web site that covers a potpourri of businesses or subjects.

One business with two or three very different products may set up two or three very different Web sites. My publisher, for example, has one site devoted only to its business guidebooks, and another site devoted to only its books about pinball machines. People visiting one of the sites has no idea the other site exists. The sites are promoted independently of each other, as though they were from two separate businesses. Both Web sites are owned by the same company, list the same street address and phone number, use the same credit card processor and the same bank account. The Web sites combine sales and expenses to figure taxes, and the company prepares one tax return. But the two Web sites enable the business to focus each site to a specialized audience.

Some people set up separate businesses, each with its own Web site. One person may own two or three businesses, all run from the same location, sharing the same mailing addresses and phone numbers, maybe using a shared credit card account. But if you want to keep your businesses legally separate, the businesses should have separate bank accounts, separate bookkeeping, and separate tax returns.

# Chapter 17:
# Web Site Host / Server

*"Everyone says they are going to revolutionize the world with a piece of software. The New Economy. I don't think there is a new economy. There are new tools for the economy. The basics of commerce remain. You've got to have something that people need, something that they can't get elsewhere. And the more they can't get it elsewhere, the more they need it."*
  **—Michael Bloomberg, Founder, Bloomberg LP, New York**

There are several ways to get your Web site online.

Very large corporations often build their own Web servers, operating their own Web sites themselves. But most businesses contract with Internet services called "Web hosts" (also called Web servers, Web hosting services, or network service providers) to "host" their Web sites; that is, put the Web sites on the Internet.

There are many, many Web hosts offering their services to businesses that want a Web site, and the hosts offer many different options. Some cost a lot of money, some are inexpensive, some are free. Some Web hosts require you, or someone you hire, to design your own site, using Web design software. Some hosts offer a "template," a pre-designed site, that only requires you to type in the text, no software required. Some Web hosts offer nothing more than space on the Web, some offer a full range of business services, including secure servers, shopping carts, and credit card processing.

The three most common options for Web hosting are (1) free or almost free Web hosting services; (2) your own ISP; (3) full service Web hosts.


## Free Web Hosting Services

Although they are disappearing fast, there are still many Web hosting services that offer free Web sites. Many of the large Web portals such as Yahoo and AltaVista offer free Web sites. Some of these sites are part of a Web "mall," a group of "stores" clustered around the site sort of like a virtual shopping mall.

On the Web, "free" is a euphemism for advertising. Free Web sites come with advertising, sometimes very annoying advertising, from companies that paid the Web server to put ads on sites, and from the Web server itself. There is no way to select the ads you want to appear on your site, and there is no way to remove the ads from your site.

Free Web sites are sometimes slow to load, and unreliable. Some search engines will not list the free sites.

These free sites are not usually full blown domains, such as www.yourbusiness.com. The domain name is usually one the Web server owns, a domain name usually starting with the Web server's site followed by the name you've chosen, such as www.YourWebHost.net/your-name-way-back-here.

It is important to distinguish between the free Web servers that provide you with a domain name that the Web server owns, and full-service Web servers that host your domain, that is, the domain name you registered and have full rights to, such as www.yourbusiness.com.

When a free Web server assigns you a domain name that includes the server's own domain name, if you leave that Web server you lose the rights to the domain name. By comparison, when a Web server hosts your own domain name, if you switch Web servers, the domain name stays with you. The domain name is yours, not the server's.

If your business has its own domain name, the name will be easier for people to remember, and it will look more professional, and maybe more trustworthy, than a domain name that is tacked onto the end of a Web server's own domain name.

Many new businesses use the free Web servers because they let you try out your Internet ideas without spending much money. You can always move your site later, to a new address, and either keep both sites or refer people from the old site to the new one.

Free Web sites may soon be a thing of the past. Web servers offered free sites, hoping to make their money off of advertising, which has not happened. As Internet service providers struggle to stay in business, as venture funds dry up, many of the free services will be eliminated. Many of the Web servers may shut down, taking your Web site with them. Keep this in mind if you are setting up a free Web site that you may have to eventually pay for or even abandon.


## Free Space From Your ISP

Most Internet Service Providers (the Internet services that connect your computer to the Internet) offer their customers a limited amount of free space on the Web for you to create and operate your own Web site. It's your space, and you can design it any way you want. The ISP does not deface your site with its own advertising. Some ISPs offer template sites, not requiring you to learn Web page software. Some ISPs expect you to have the software to design your own site or to hire a Web designer.

An ISP-sponsored Web site belongs to the ISP, and is only available to you as long as you are a customer of that ISP. The Web address will include your ISP's name at the beginning of the address, resulting in a long and impossible to remember domain name.

Many successful Internet businesses use their ISP's free space and are quite happy with the results. These businesses don't expect people to remember their domain name. The sites rely on search engines and links from other sites. Links are discussed in **Chapter 18: Web Site Design**.

Your ISP also probably offers full service Web hosting, with your own domain name. This, however, is not a free service. But since you already are paying the ISP for your Internet connection, the ISP may have a very attractive rate structure for subscribers. Compare your ISP's packages and prices with full-service Web hosts.


## Full-Service Web Hosting

For a fee ranging from about $25 a month on up, a full-service Web host can offer just about any Web service and any features you want to pay for. Many hosting services offer packages, bundled services, at different prices.

Investigate Web hosting services carefully. Compare services and prices. Don't sign a long-term contract unless you are completely confident about your host's ability to deliver what's promised. Your Web site is yours, so if you do not like your hosting service, you can switch to another host without having to change your Web address.

Many hosting services advertise in business magazines and on the Web, or you can ask for recommendations from people you know who already have Web sites. Some important issues:

1. First, and most important, do not let your Web host register your domain name for you. Do it yourself. Sign up directly with a domain name registrar, and renew your domain yourself through the registrar. Don't agree to any "free domain registration" offers. I have heard too many sad stories about businesses that discovered, too late, that their Web hosting service claimed ownership of domain names they registered for client businesses. When unhappy businesses tried to move to a new Web host, the businesses were shocked to discover they did not own their domain name, and that the Web hosting service would not give them or sell them their domain name.

2. Make sure the host is "transparent," invisible to your site's visitors. No ads, no links, no "hosted by" messages.

3. Pick a Web host that looks like it has staying power, one with ample resources, not likely to close their doors without warning. If the Web host will provide with you a list of its clients, contact the clients and ask if they are happy with the host's services.

4. Ask about the Web host's restrictions on your Web site activities. Can the host cancel your contract if they do not like the content of your site, or if you attract too many visitors, or if you send or receive a lot of e-mail? Will the host charge you more per month if your traffic increases?

5. Ask about downtime and technical problems. Does the host have a poor record of breakdowns? Is the host monitoring its systems 24 hours a day? Does the host have a back-up generator if the power goes out? Is the host prepared in case of a technical emergency or a natural disaster?

6. Can the Web host accommodate the software you want to use on your

Web site? Some servers are not set up to support some types of Web programming software.

7. Does the Web host offer a secure system (called a "secure server") for credit card transactions and transmission of private data? Is the system flexible, with different options? This is an area of Web hosting that requires careful examination on your part, if you plan to make sales over the Internet. It is discussed in **Chapter 25: Online Payment Systems**.

8. How is the host prepared to deal with hackers and other breaches of security? Does the host have procedures that keep unauthorized people from getting into your Web site or obtaining technical information about your site? Does the host have insurance or a bond to cover you should a security lapse cause you or your customers financial loss or other problems?

9. Is the host located in a state that is trying to demand sales tax collections from the host's customers? See **Chapter 29: Taxes** for more about this possible problem.

10. If you want to transfer to another hosting service, or if your hosting service goes bankrupt, will you be able to gain access to your site?

11. Read ALL the fine print in the contract (sometimes called a "Terms of Service" or "Terms of Use" agreement). Every word in the Web host's contract is there to protect the host, to limit its liability. Be very careful if the contract states that you indemnify the host against any problems caused by your Web site. "Indemnify" means that you agree to pay the host's attorney fees and court costs if there is a lawsuit. You can ask to have a contract modified to meet your own requirements, but your request will probably be denied. It's up to you to decide what you can live with. Once you click on the "I accept" button, you have made a legal, binding contract. Be sure you know exactly what you've agreed to.

## Chapter 18:
# Web Site Design

*"A Web site's design reinforces either the perception that a company has a solid e-strategy or that it doesn't know what it is doing."*
**—Matt Cutler, Co-Founder, Netgenesis**

There are dozens upon dozens of books about Web site design. Every business magazine has an article almost every issue on Web site design. The more you read, and the more you study other people's Web sites, the better your Web site will be.

When I give retail seminars, for people opening new retail stores, I always suggest that they visit as many retail stores as they can. Look at how other people have designed their stores. Notice what you like about the stores, and notice what you don't like about the stores. Use what you learn to design your own store.

The same suggestions apply to designing a Web site. Study Web sites. There are millions of sites out there you can learn from, just by visiting them. Note what it is you like about some sites and dislike about others. Take detailed notes. And design your site based on what you learn.

I am not a Web site designer, although like every other site owner, I've given it a try. I do not know Web design software very well. I hired someone to do that for me. But I do know some important considerations when designing a Web site:

1. People always have, and always will, judge you by your appearance. A good looking paint job helps to sell a car, a good looking cover helps to sell a book, a good looking Web site helps to sell a business. Your site must look good and must look professional. An attractive, professional looking site instills trust in consumers who don't know you.

2. Your Web site must download fast. People have little patience for slow loading Web sites. Keep in mind that many people have old computers and slow modems, and these will make a slow loading site even slower. People have old, low-resolution monitors. Large graphics, video, and other flashy

software are the main cause of slow loading sites. A good Web site designer knows how to code graphics so they load fast.

3. Make your site easy to understand, easy to navigate. The best Web sites help people quickly find the information they want. People have no tolerance for confusing, complicated sites. People like sites that are "intuitive," that is, sites people can figure out without reading the instructions.

4. Avoid decorative clutter, inconsistent layout, jumbled typefaces, random designs. People are moving fast on the Internet and will quickly abandon a site that slows them down, that confuses them, or makes them wade through useless stuff.

5. Avoid color combinations and background designs that make reading difficult. Many people have trouble reading dark type on a dark background, light type on a light background, and words typed on top of checkered or "busy" backgrounds.

6. A flashy presentation sometimes impresses first time visitors, but it may grow to annoy repeat visitors. Have a series of buttons at the top of your home page, buttons that load quickly, so repeat visitors can go immediately to the information they're looking for.

7. Every page on your site should have a link that takes the visitor back to your home page. Quite often, someone using a search engine will find one of your pages but not your home page. Someone who is directed to the middle of your site by a search engine might get confused if your site does not make it clear on every page who you are, how to reach you, and how to find your home page.

8. Keep Web pages short if possible, and keep the text narrow. People do not like to scroll down too far, and they hate having to scroll back and forth, and back and forth, to read lines that are too long for their screen.

9. Consider offering a "text only" option on your site, for people with older computers and very slow Internet access. Blind Web surfers have software

that can read text-only sites out loud. Although the text-only version will not look anywhere as good as your regular site, it may bring in visitors who otherwise can't access your site.

10. Do not underestimate the importance of good grammar, correct spelling, proper sentence structure, and all that other stuff you didn't learn in high school. People who know good English when they see it will be critical (and possibly distrustful) of a Web site that uses bad English. Much more important, however, poor grammar makes sentences harder to read and harder to understand. Bad grammar = Miscommunication. If you are not good at English composition, find someone to edit the content of your site.

11. Check your site from other computers using other operating systems, other Internet access providers, and other browsers, to see if the site works for everybody trying to access it. I have discovered sites that load fine on Internet Explorer but will not load on Netscape. Also, if possible, check your Web site using older versions of Netscape and Internet Explorer. Many people do not update the browsers and have older versions. The problem of browser incompatibility is in the site's programming, something an experienced site designer can correct. I have found sites that look good on some computers but look all jumbled on others. This again is a programming flaw, a sign of an inexperienced programmer.

12. Ask friends to "test drive" your site, navigate the entire site, and look for flaws, problems, and things that might confuse people. Try especially to find someone who is not an experienced Internet user, someone who does not already know tricks for navigating Web sites. If a novice Web surfer can use and understand your site, you will turn many more visitors into customers. A huge percentage of visitors leave sites solely because the visitors cannot figure out how to use the sites.

13. Check your site every day. Make sure your server has it up and running properly, make sure no error messages have suddenly appeared.

14. If you want repeat customers, change things on your site regularly, just as a retail store changes what's in the window. Let customers know what's

new. Create a mini-newsletter or develop an "Ask the expert" column. Keep your site current; if you have a holiday theme, don't forget to take it down after the holiday.

15. The best Web sites solicit feedback from visitors, particularly complaints about the site, and use that feedback to improve the site, making it easier to use, rewording instructions, adding new features. Show your e-mail address prominently on your site and encourage visitors to contact you. Make sure the visitor can simply click on your e-mail address and automatically have a pre-addressed e-mail dialog box, ready and waiting (see below). Check your e-mail regularly. A same-day reply will increase the likelihood your visitors will become customers.

16. Web surfers often mistrust Internet businesses they don't know or can't check on. If you've been in business for a few years, or if you have credentials that sound impressive, brag a little, let people know about it. Include your telephone and fax numbers, and a mailing address, to help visitors feel confident that they are dealing with a legitimate business. You may want to include the phone number on every page. Some people print out a page from your Web site and then can't remember how to contact you. Contact information on every page will solve this problem. If you list a toll free number, be sure to include your regular phone number as well. Toll free numbers often can't be accessed by people outside the United States.

17. Don't force people to register on your Web site or give out personal information unless they are placing an order. If you ask for personal information, you will lose most of your visitors.

18. Buyers want to know up front how much an item really costs, including shipping. Too many sites don't show shipping charges until after the customer fills in the order form. If you force customers to fill in their orders before telling them how much shipping will cost them, you will lose many customers.

## Meta-Tags

Meta-tags are hidden words and phrases Web designers bury in Web sites. Meta-tags describe the contents of the sites. Meta-tags are invisible. No one who visits your site sees the meta tags. But some some search engines use the hidden meta tags as part of their selection process, determining what sites get good listings and what sites don't. There is a real skill to carefully picking meta-tags. You should either learn about meta-tags or hire a designer who knows how to choose the best meta-tags for your site.

## Starting With a Simple Site

If you are just testing the Internet waters, I suggest you start with a site that is simple and basic, something you can have up and running quickly, and expand from there.

You can start with a very easy-to-build Web site, often called a "billboard," "brochure," or "static" site, where your visitors get to look at your site, contact you by e-mail, and place orders offline by mail or telephone. From there you can add online ordering, product searches, and other interactive options.

Web sites can be designed and modified and remodified, constantly if necessary, until you hit on a formula that works. The most successful Web businesses see their sites as perpetual works in progress. Don't be afraid to experiment with your site.

One advantage that Web sites have over printed catalogs and retail stores is the ability to try a new design or a new offer, with little cost, and see near-immediate results. What happens if you offer a 10% discount versus a 5% discount or no discount at all? You can test your prices quickly, sometimes within a few hours, and keep revising your offers until you find out what works. Try offering free shipping, and see if sales increase. What if you offer free gift wrapping? If you suspect that an offer of free gift wrap might boost sales, you can test that idea online for a few days, and measure the results before investing in truckloads of gift wrap.

Don't be discouraged if your Web site is not coming together quite the way it should. The technology does not always work as smoothly as you'd like. It is easy to let all of these Web suggestions, all of the possibilities for your site, overwhelm you, and scare you away from designing a site and getting it operational.

Just take your time, and make sure your site is operating the way you want it before you tell everyone about it. Once you are satisfied with the site, include the Web address (your domain name) on all advertisements, business cards, stationery, etc.


## E-Mail From A Web Site

Business Web sites let visitors e-mail the business directly from the site. The visitor never has to log off the site to send you an e-mail.

Most Web sites use an e-mail address that includes the name of the Web site, the domain name. For example, if your domain name is www.buystuff.com, your e-mail can be sent to you@buystuff.com, or to info@buystuff.com, catalog@buystuff.com, newsletter@buystuff.com, or any-other-name-you-want@buystuff.com. You can have several e-mail names @buystuff.com.

All of the different e-mail names @buystuff.com are actually sent to one e-mail address. The e-mail is sent to your regular e-mail address at your regular ISP. Even though your ISP does not host your Web site, the e-mail is still routed to you through your ISP. This is known as an e-mail "alias." It is a seamless operation, invisible to the Web visitor.

An e-mail address through your own Web site has a professional appearance, and makes it easy for customers to remember your e-mail address. An e-mail address through your Web site also eliminates the problem of losing your e-mail address if you switch ISPs. The Web site can direct e-mail from the site to any ISP you choose.


## Links

Links from other Web sites will bring more visitors to your site. A link is very much like a recommendation, like word-of-mouth publicity, and usually costs nothing.

Let me give you a real life example. My publisher, Bell Springs Publishing, publishes a pinball machine repair book, which appeals to a small but very eager group of people. Bell Springs set up a separate Web page just for that one book (www.aboutpinball.com). The publisher then went surfing the Internet, using search engines, and found several hundred Web sites about pinball. Some were businesses, many were individuals with little home pages about their favorite hobby. My publisher e-mailed every site she found, requesting a link to the pinball book's site. Many of the sites happily agreed. The links brought many additional visitors to the Web site.

Links have an extra benefit. Search engines often find a link to a Web site rather than Web site itself. It is effortless for a Web surfer, led to a link, to click on the link and get rerouted to your site.

## Legal Problems With Links

If you include a link to another site on your own site, the link may cause you problems. Some Web sites do not want to be linked to others, and strictly forbid it in the terms posted on their sites. Sites that are linked without their approval have been known to claim copyright infringement, or even trespassing, against the site offering the link. Sites that have legal requirements for entry, requiring visitors to click on an approval button, may claim breach-of-contract infringement if your link to their site bypasses the approval button.

Some sites are concerned that viewers will think the link is your site, and not their site. This is especially true if the link leads your visitors to a page within someone else's site and not to that site's home page. This is known as "deep linking," and makes it very easy to mislead viewers as to who's site they are actually viewing.

This is an untested and questionable area of law. But you don't want to be the one doing the test, and there is nothing to be gained by angering the owners of a site. If you link another site to yours, I suggest you ask their permission. When you get an okay, keep a written copy.

Want to know more link-related problems? If you are linked to a site that has libelous, objectionable or illegal material on it, your site could be implicated. Generally, the courts hold that third party sites can be liable for contents of a linked site, if the third party knew, or should have known, that the linked site contained infringing or illegal material.

This "third party" liability is a rare situation, and easily avoided. This situation might occur only if you include a link to a "problem" site on your own site. It's always a good idea to periodically check any links you include on your site.

Generally, you are not held responsible for another site's contents if that site includes your site as a link. But if you find your Web site listed as a link on someone else's Web site that you find questionable or problematical, send an e-mail and request that the link be removed. Keep a copy of your e-mail should you ever be questioned about your connection to the problem site.

---

# Chapter 19:
# Web Designer Contract

*"Entrepreneurs confuse what's technologically possible with what buyers actually want."*
**—Peter Coy, Business Week Magazine**

If you hire a web designer, either an individual or a company, it is of utmost importance that you and the designer have a written agreement that states very clearly what is to be accomplished. Before you write up an agreement, verbally discuss the extent of the work, the time frame and the cost. Make sure you are both "on the same page," as they say in California. That is, you agree on the basics. The web designer, if he or she is an experienced professional, may already have a contract prepared. Keep in mind that contracts usually favor the person who wrote them. Read the contract thoroughly, and ask about any clauses you do not understand. Do not hesitate to ask for changes if you do not like the agreement.

## Ownership of the Work

Who owns the rights to the work the designer is doing: the words, the illustrations, the layout and design of the Web pages, the coding, everything?

Do not unintentionally put yourself in a situation where the designer owns the content or design of your Web site. The law is very clear: the creator of a work—a book, a song, an advertisement, a Web page—is the legal owner of that work, unless you have a written agreement with the designer that grants you the rights to the work, or unless the designer is your employee, on your payroll. (Freelance designers are *not* employees, explained below).

This is your web site, your business, your livelihood, and your money invested in having the site designed. You want to have full ownership and all rights to the completed work. You want to have it copyrighted in your name, or in the name of your business.

Once you pay the designer for the work, you want to be sure, and you want the designer to understand, that ownership of the work is 100% yours. The designer is not entitled to any future royalties or other payments. The designer may not reuse the work for himself or for another client. The designer may not make any future demand on what you can or cannot do with your site.

There are designers who will balk at this arrangement, designers who want to retain full or part ownership of their work, designers who want to copyright the work in their own name. I suggest that you do not work with these people. There are many, many Web design companies and freelancers. You should have no trouble finding a designer who agrees to your terms. But, again, get it in writing.

## Legal Status of Designer: Independent Contractor

Next, you may want to discuss the designer's legal status. If you are hiring a web design company or a self-employed freelance designer, there is no question that you are hiring what the IRS calls an "independent contractor." An independent contractor is someone who is self-employed, has a legal business, files business tax returns, and pays his or her own income and payroll taxes.

In other words, the designer is not your employee. You are not an employer. You are hiring a professional to do a job and go away when the job is done, much as you would hire an accountant to prepare your taxes or a lawyer to draft incorporation papers, or a plumber to fix the sink. You are not responsible for withholding the employee taxes, paying employer taxes, workers compensation insurance, unemployment insurance, or any of the other the other laws and regulations required of employers.

If the designer is someone with no professional background, no clients, no business licenses, no idea what a business tax return looks like (hey, some of the best Web designers meet this description), you need to make it clear to the designer, and put it in writing, that this job is freelance, one time only, not employment. The designer must understand that you are not hiring an employee, that there is no unemployment insurance when the job is over, that the designer is responsible for his own taxes, insurance, and everything else.

This is for your own protection. The IRS is forever suspicious of employers evading payroll taxes by disguising employees as independent contractors. And legal nightmares can explode if an undocumented and uninsured employee is injured on the job. Your contract with the Web designer will go a long way towards alleviating these problems, although you still ought to have business liability insurance if your designer, or any-one else, is injured while on your business premises. This is covered in **Chapter 11: Insurance for Internet Businesses**.

## Fees

All financial aspects of the contract should be discussed in detail, in advance. Don't be embarrassed to talk money, don't leave it to "we'll work it out later." There are many variables when it comes to designing a web site, hours spent that may not produce the results you want, work that may require fine tuning or even starting all over.

Do you pay the designer a flat fee for a complete job, finished to your satisfaction, and paid for only when the job is done? That by far would be your best deal, I think, but the designer may not care for such a contract that leaves him vulnerable to not getting paid.

Do you pay by the hour, no matter how many hours are spent, no matter what the results are? Do you set a maximum number of hours? Do you pay a deposit? Do you pay in installments? Do you set deadlines for completing the work. What if the deadlines are missed? Does your contract include an agreement for ongoing help from the designer, after the Web site is designed and online? All of these details should be in writing, part of the contract. If you leave them to chance, chance is you'll wish you hadn't.

More information about contracts: **Chapter 28: Law By Contract**.

# Chapter 20:
# Security

*"There's definitely a psychological sense of fear out there. People think their information will be sucked out of their computer and posted on someone's Web site."*
**—Marcus Roberts, CEO, Clickbuytel**

Nothing on the Internet is 100% secure. Web site owners should take as many reasonable precautions as possible.

Limit access to your computer. If employees or others will be using your computer, establish passwords that let people only into the areas you want them to be able to access. Change the passwords every 60 or 90 days. Lock the door when you are not around.

Don't leave your Internet connection on all the time. A sitting, Internet-connected computer gives hackers lots of time to try to break in. This is a greater problem for businesses with broadband, cable, and DSL (digital subscriber line) connections, which have the capacity to be always on. If your Internet connection is always on, turn off your computer when not using it.

Do not store your customers' personal information on your Web site. Once a transaction is complete, move the information offline. This way, should anyone gain unauthorized access to your site, there will be no credit card numbers and other private customer information to steal.

Don't download files from chat-room strangers. Do not download software from an unreliable source.

Occasionally check the Web sites of the companies that provide your browser, your e-mail program, and your other Internet software to see if the software has been updated. Software updates often include security fixes. You can usually download the updates for free or for a small fee.

A law called the Financial Services Modernization Act, also called the Gramm-Leach-Bliley Act, requires financial institutions to have secure Web sites, conduct risk assessments, and protect their information from "threats, hazards, and unauthorized access." The act does not define with a "financial institution" is, but most lawyers agree that it only covers banks and similar financial lenders.

## E-Mail

This was already covered in Section One, but it bears repeating. E-mail is not secure. E-mail can easily be read by others, forwarded, copied, printed out, and saved by the sender and recipient. E-mail, if not deleted, can linger in a computer's hard drive for years. Do not send anything by e-mail that demands security or might cause you a problem with privacy. Delete sensitive information as soon as possible.

## Computer Virus

A computer virus is a piece of uninvited, unwelcome programming, created by some computer genius with a warped mind. A virus can cause minor or serious problems with your computer. It can alter or destroy data.

A virus can enter your computer if you load an infected disk, and can be transferred to another computer that loads an infected disk from your computer. Viruses can sometimes, though rarely, enter your computer from a Web site you visit, or from someone breaking into your own Web site. Viruses can enter your computer when you download booby-trapped software from the Internet. Be cautious of any software offered by someone you don't know.

Most viruses enter computers through e-mail. The creator of a virus can e-mail someone, anyone, with the virus hidden in the e-mail message. Viruses are often hidden in e-mail "attachments." Look out for the paperclip logo! When you open the attachment, the virus is set loose in your computer. The virus can then travel to anyone who you e-mail.

Some really nasty viruses automatically mail themselves to everyone in the infected computer's address book or database. The virus actually self e-mails itself to all of your friends and business contacts, and says the e-mail is from you! How's that for a PR nightmare? And if the recipient opens the attachment, the virus is set loose in the recipient's computer, and the virus continues its spread, sometimes all over the world, in just a few hours.

## Virus Protection Software

If you do not already have virus protection software, get it today. You can buy software in a box and install it yourself, or buy it from a computer dealer who will install it for you, or buy it off the Internet and download it.

The software usually comes with free updates for a year, downloaded from the Internet. The company that makes the software will notify you every week, or however often you indicate, that it is time to update your software. New viruses show up all the time, so it is essential that your anti-virus software stays current.

## Additional Virus Protection

Don't rely exclusively on virus protection software. The software is not always 100% effective. Sometimes a new virus hits before the software company has come up with the antidote. Sometimes a new virus appears before you've updated the anti-virus software on your hard drive.

Take your own precautions. Never open an e-mail attachment unless you know exactly what it is, you know ahead of time that someone is sending you an attachment, and you are expecting it. Even if the sender is someone you know and trust, don't open the attachment if you don't know what it is. The sender may have not sent the e-mail. The virus may have sent the e-mail. Does this sound like some Hollywood horror movie?

Do not send e-mail attachments to anyone without first getting their permission. People have learned to be very suspicious of attachments. No point in adding suspicion and worry to your business dealings.

If you have employees, make sure they practice safe e-mail. (Sorry).

If your computer contracts a virus, it may be easy or difficult to eliminate. Your Internet Service Provider, or your Web host, or a local computer store may be able to tell you how to clean your hard drive, if it is a simple operation. Or you may have to take your computer to someone who specializes in computer problems. Most likely, a local computer store can help you. It will not cost a lot of money, but it is essential that it be done.

Since some viruses self-mail to people in your address book, you may want to eliminate or pare down the list. Every e-mail program has an address book, and every e-mail you send is automatically added to the address book. There could be several hundred names in there and you don't even know it. If you don't use the address book, you can disable it. You can also go into your address book periodically, and remove addresses you no longer need.

## Firewalls

You can purchase what is called "firewall" software or hardware, which protects your computer from unauthorized intrusions. Firewalls make it very difficult for hackers to break into your computer or into your Web site.

Firewall software is especially beneficial, some people say essential, if you have an always-on Internet connection such as cable or DSL. An always-on connection is much more vulnerable to a hacker's attack than if you have a regular dial-up connection that you log onto and log off.

## A Separate Computer

Some businesses use a separate computer, or a separate hard drive, for e-mail and Internet connections. All of the company's files and working programs are kept on a computer (or hard drive) with no Internet access. This way, any virus that may come through the Internet will not damage or expose any of the company's records.

---

# Chapter 21:
# When Your Web Site Goes Down

*"It's all automated. It's a thorough system that organizes responses. There are things like Keep Doing Your Best, Work Hard. It's canned responses. There are over 25 possible responses from Santa."*
**—Craig Kronenberger, founder, www.claus.com**

What happens one day when a customer tries to access your site and nothing is there but a message saying that the page can't be found? It happens. As far as the customer knows, you could be out of business.

Web sites go down for any number of reasons, and sometimes for good ones. Web servers are just big computers. They need occasional maintenance and like any other machine, they can break down. Usually the maintenance is scheduled late at night and takes just a few minutes.

Occasionally, something unexpected comes up during the day but can still be handled quickly. It may be that a virus strikes, or a site owner uploads a script with bugs that temporarily overloads the system.

A problem may be caused by other Web sites on the server. Most Web sites are on shared servers: several sites (yours and others) share a single large server, sharing the available space, sharing all the problems the server may encounter.

If one site on the server experiences an unusually high volume of traffic, it can adversely affect your site. If a hacker breaks into a site on the server, it could disrupt all the sites on the server, including yours.

The trouble comes when your Web site goes down for a significant amount of time during high traffic hours. Storms, power outages, earthquakes and other natural and man-made disasters cannot be anticipated. Your Web host should have surge protectors, backup systems, and all kinds of protective measures in place. But nothing can protect the servers from the full force of a major disruption.

The worst possible problem that can happen comes from your Web host itself. It can go bankrupt, pull the plug, and disappear—along with your site, and any e-mail coming through your site.


## What To Do When Your Web Site Disappears

The first thing to do is make sure there really is a problem with the Web site. Before you panic, try going to other Web sites. If you can't reach any other Web sites, your Internet connection is down, not your Web server.

If you have just updated your Web site, try accessing it with different browsers. You may have inadvertently put up a page with coding that your browser (Netscape or Internet Explorer) is unable to read.

Try accessing your site from other computers, and from other ISPs. Call a couple friends and ask them to try to access your site. Make sure the problem is with your site and not with your own computer.

If it appears that the problem is with your Web server, call your Web host and report the problem. More likely than not, they are aware of the problem and working to fix it. But there is the possibility they are not aware of the problem yet.

The Web host should be able to give you some estimate of the time your site will be down.

## Backup (Mirror) Site

Many businesses have a "mirror" site, a second, back-up Web site, usually small, just a duplication of your home page. Businesses set up backup sites with one or more of the free hosting services on the Internet, or on the free space most ISPs give their clients.

Your Web host may be able to redirect people to your back-up site If not, the only way you can direct people to the back up site is to notify them by phone or e-mail.

You should e-mail all of your regular customers. Put together a short message. Assure your customers that your regular site will be up again soon, and invite them to visit the mirror site. Give them a back-up e-mail address where they can reach you. E-mail addressed through the non-working site (you@www.yourbusiness.com) will most likely not be deliverable. Maybe even take advantage of the situation and offer a special discount on your products.

Back-up sites usually have a link to your regular Web site. In the event of a failure of your main site, remove the links on the back-up site, so people accessing the back-up site won't try to access your main site.

Once your main Web site is operating again, you may want to again send an e-mail to your customers (and maybe send a press release to the media) announcing that the problem was quickly solved, and you are back in business. Promote your business a little, and turn the potentially damaging downtime into an opportunity to get some good publicity.

Don't forget to go to the mirror site and reinstall the links you removed while your main site was down. You may want to add a temporary notice that your main site is working again.

## Be Prepared

1. Check your site every day. Consider installing both Netscape and Internet Explorer, so you can check your site from both browsers. You can get Netscape's browser from **www.netscape.com**. You can get Explorer from **www.microsoft.com**.

2. Have one or more mirror sites up and running.

3. Keep a full back-up of your Web site on CD, tape, disk, or other off-computer storage, just as you keep a back-up of your other computer files (okay, back up the Web site *and* the other files you've been meaning to back up). When you update your site, don't forget to update the back-up also.

4. Keep phone numbers, account numbers, and contact names for your Web hosting service at hand, so you can contact them immediately.

5. Have an up-to-date e-mail list of all important customers, media, and others who regularly access your site, so you can notify them.

6. If staying online is vital to your business, you may want to sign up with a service that will monitor your site and notify you of downtime. Some of these services are free, some cost money. Your Web host or Web site designer can probably recommend a service, or use a search engine to find one.

7. Get and keep receipts for all fees paid to your Web host. The number one reason Web sites go down is because they are behind in payments—or the host thinks they are behind in payments, because a payment was not recorded correctly. Don't assume that just because you sent in a check, the people on the other end have credited your account. They are usually better at running computers than accounting.

8. Finally, don't panic. Even the biggest Internet sites go down from time to time. The Internet is young. It's a miracle it works as well as it does. If

you have no control over the situation, do what you can from your end, and take the rest of the day off. *"Mama said there'd be days like this."*

---

## Chapter 22:
# Web Site Pirates and Troublemakers

*"If it can happen there it can happen anywhere: Last October Microsoft discovered that hackers had infiltrated the company's network. Evidence suggests that the unidentified hackers had access for three months before they were detected."*
**—Reported in Small Business Computing Magazine**

Small Internet businesses do not usually have problems with malicious hoodlums trying to damage the Web site or cause trouble for the business. The hackers and criminals that go after Web sites target large Internet businesses, where there is a lot of publicity and a lot of money. But should you find yourself attacked or blackmailed by some Internet troublemaker, there are several ways to proceed.

The days of "cybersquatting" and "cyberpiracy" are mostly over. This was a common situation in the early days of domain names, where some fast-buck artist would register a business's name or brand name or trademark, and then demand ransom money to sell the domain name to the business. Federal law now prohibits people from registering a domain name that is someone else's registered trademark.

If a cybersquatter registers a domain name that is similar to yours, in an attempt to deceive people into thinking that the domain is really yours (called "typo-squatting"), this is fraud and it also is prohibited by law.

Domain names that make fun of or parody other domain names are not prohibited by law, and are almost impossible to stop. The best thing you can do is just ignore the parody site. Few Web surfers are likely to find it anyway. People who set up such sites are often looking for attention. When they get none, their interest flags, and the sites eventually disappear.

If a site is libeling you or spreading false information, you have a legal right to demand that the site owner remove the false information. You can also contact the Web host for the site and demand that the Web host shut down the site. Web hosts do not want to be caught up in such disputes and will often take action. If you look up the offending Web site on a "who-is" search (see **Chapter 16: Domain Names**) the Web host will be listed.

---

# Chapter 23
# Search Engines

*"Business is war. Upgrade your trenches."*
        **—Magazine advertisement for Inter Continental Hotels**

All Web surfers use search engines to find what they're looking for. Getting your business listed on search engines can make the difference between success and failure.

Every Internet business wants to be in the Top Five or Top Ten listings, but there are 32 million Web sites out there. How you design your Web site, and how you notify the search engines, will have a major impact on your search engine listings.

Your Web site won't just magically appear on search engines when you launch your site. Your site may not show up for a month or two or three, or may not show up at all, unless you do research, learn how the different search engines work and how to submit your site to the search engines.

There is no standard formula to getting a good listing on search engines. Each search engine works a little (or a lot) differently than every other search engine. Search engines keep their methods secret, and they often modify their methods.

Most search engines allow you to submit your Web for consideration. Submitting your site in no way guarantees a search engine listing, but if you don't submit the site, many search engines will not even consider you. Log onto every search engine you can find, especially the major search engines, and go to their "submit" page or form, and follow their instructions.

Some search engines look at the hidden meta-tags (see **Meta Tags** above) in rating Web sites, some search engines look at the first few words on your home page, some search engines examine your entire site.

A good Web designer will know how the major search engines work. The designer will know how to design your site to make it more likely to get a good listing on search engines. When considering different Web designers, you might want to see if the designer's other clients have good search engine placement.

A new, and troublesome, trend in search engine placement is "pay to play:" paying for a top listing. All of the major search engines are adding this "buy a Top Five listing" option. Some search engines make it very clear to Web surfers that the top listings were bought, some search engines are less than forthcoming in disclosing this information.

As more and more businesses buy their way onto search engines, the entire concept of Web commerce is likely to change. Small Internet businesses that cannot afford to buy a listing will be at a great disadvantage. Web surfers may or may not be happy with the concept of search-engine "Yellow Pages" instead of the present "let's see what's out there" free-for-all. The result may well be two types of search engines: those that only list businesses that pay for listings; and those that list everything they can find on the Internet, possibly charging Web surfers a monthly subscription fee, or a fee per search.

Of all the bramble patches in the field of Internet business, this one could well be the thorniest. Your business needs the search engines, but search engines don't need you. They'll be calling the shots. As the search engines find the revenue models that work for them, you will have to make sure your business is included.

**"You're naive if you think people will come back to your site because they like it. Ten minutes after they've been there, they've forgotten about it. Solve that problem. Design your site so visitors can voluntarily leave their e-mail address behind. That's what big companies count on, repeat business, created through inexpensive e-mail direct marketing. It's a trick even the smallest business can profit from."**

—*Tom Antion, Web business consultant*

# Section Four:
# E-Commerce

*"For any business, large or small, not to have an e-commerce strategy is a big mistake."*
—William Daley,
Former Secretary of Commerce

# Chapter 24:
# E-Commerce

*"Before you spend a fortune implementing a database solution for your e-business, you might want to take an extra day to weigh your options. The adage 'measure twice, cut once' has worked for a few thousand years. The New Economy won't displace the old rules."*
**—Joey Trimyer, Vice President, FormFill, Austin, Texas**

Why does any business have a Web site? Dumb question, I guess. But how many business Web sites have you visited that you couldn't quite figure out what the site was doing there, what the business was trying to convey, if you could purchase anything from the company, and how?

Most commercial Web sites are there to find new customers, keep old customers, and make sales. The businesses that own the sites must figure out how to successfully conduct business from their sites.

The simplest sites do not take orders directly over the Internet. The sites are much like mail order catalogs. These catalog or "billboard" sites, as they are often called, include contact information on the site: phone, fax, address. Customers find what they want on the site, and then phone, mail, or fax an order to the company.

Many of these billboard sites include an order form the customer can print out, and then mail or fax to the business, just like an order form in a catalog. Some order forms require the customer to write in all the information by hand after printing out the form. Some order forms can be filled out online, but still must be printed out, and then mailed or faxed.

The next step up for a business Web site is an online payment system. Customers can place orders directly from the site. This gets to the heart of Internet commerce, making the best use of the Web to encourage your customers to order online, right here, right now.

The term "e-commerce" refers to business conducted online, online purchasing as opposed to finding what you want on a Web site and then ordering offline. E-commerce cannot exist without online payment systems.

# Chapter 25:
# Online Payment Systems

*"People are not going to the Internet because they perceive it's cheaper. They go because they can't find what they want elsewhere. They go because they don't want to shop in twelve stores."*
                    **—Jeffrey Cole, University of California, Los Angeles**

There are several ways to take payment for online orders. For retail sales (that is, not business-to-business sales), most people who purchase online use credit cards: VISA, MasterCard, American Express, or Discover. If you are not set up to accept credit cards, you will be at a great disadvantage.

There are two ways you can accept credit card orders: through your own merchant account, or through a third-party processor.

## Your Own Merchant Account

Most established merchants have a credit card account (called a "merchant account" or "merchant status") through their bank. You do not apply directly to VISA or MasterCard to become a credit-card merchant. You go through a bank or through a third-party credit card processor (discussed below). Banks also process American Express and Discover cards, but you sign up for these cards directly with American Express and Discover.

Banks are very choosy about who they will set up as a credit-card merchant. Visible public operations, such as retail stores, usually have no trouble getting credit-card merchant status. But new Internet businesses, mail order businesses, and home businesses are often turned down. Too many fraudulent scams and here-today-gone-tomorrow entrepreneurs have cost the banks too much money. The Internet in particular has a much higher fraud rate than other forms of business, and banks are exceptionally leery of Internet-only businesses.

If you've been in business a few years or if you have a good relationship with a bank, you are more likely to be approved. Keep in mind that the bank, not the credit card company, decides who gets merchant status. So if one bank turns you down, try another (and *another*). Also try local thrifts and credit unions. Some of these institutions offer merchant credit card accounts.

Some businesses that are turned down by banks get a merchant account through third-party service bureaus, sometimes called processing centers or independent sales organizations (ISOs). Some of these operations, however, are excessively expensive or downright fraudulent. Be very cautious of these people, especially if they want money up-front to "process" or "evaluate" your application. Find out what bank they are affiliated with, and check with VISA and MasterCard to find out if the ISO is properly registered.

You might also join a trade or business association that offers a credit card service.

## Credit Card Fees

Fees for setting you up as a credit card merchant and for processing your transactions can vary, often dramatically, depending on where you get your merchant status (bank or ISO), dollar volume, and number of transactions a month.

For small accounts, banks typically charge 3% to 4% of the sale amount. Some banks and ISOs also have a minimum monthly fee, or a per-transaction fee, in addition to the 3-4% they deduct from your sales.

## Charge-Backs

Merchants who accept credit cards in person—where someone hands you the card, you compare signatures, check expiration date, and immediately process the card to see if it will be accepted or rejected—are usually not held responsible for stolen or invalid cards.

If you are taking credit card orders over Internet, telephone, or fax, banks will not accept any responsibility for invalid, fraudulent or stolen credit cards that were processed in what they call "card not present" transactions. Even if your credit card terminal accepts the sale and gives you an approval, there is no guarantee that you won't get charged back if there is a problem with the card.

Even if the credit-card transaction is legitimate, if your customer refuses to pay your bill for any plausible reason, claiming that the merchandise was never received, or it was damaged, or it was returned, or never even ordered, the bank will side with the customer every time. If the dispute is not resolved to the customer's satisfaction, the bank will charge back your account, and there is little or nothing you'll be able to do about it.

## Third Party Credit Card Processor

Internet businesses that cannot get merchant status can still accept credit cards on their Web sites, by working with an online credit card service, one that processes your credit card orders for you. When your customer clicks on the "order" button on your Web site, the customer is automatically transferred to a Web site belonging to the credit card service. Your customer is actually billed by the online credit-card service, not by your business. The billing company then sends you the money, less the fees the service charges you.

Some customers may be scared off by finding themselves dealing with a different company than the one they thought they were buying from. Many experienced Web buyers, however, are familiar with this system and very comfortable with it, especially if the credit card processor is a large company with a well-known name.

Different credit card services have different procedures. Some hold back payment to you for a period of time, to be sure your customer pays the bill, and that there isn't a dispute between you and your customer. Find out how the credit card processor handles returns and charge-backs. Find out who is responsible for fraudulent orders.

Many Web hosts offer credit-card processing as an option, as part of the hosting package. Internet credit card processors advertise widely in business magazines and on the Internet. You can type in "accept credit cards" in a search engine and get a list of businesses offering this service.

Before signing up with a credit card processor, get a list of their clients, and check out the clients' Web sites. See how the sites look and operate. Start the process of buying something from the client's site, and see how smoothly it goes. You can cancel the order before actually submitting it.

## Online Ordering: Shopping Carts

The most common way to take online orders is through what's called a "shopping cart." This isn't a cart at all, but a software system for taking credit-card orders over the Internet. It's called a shopping cart because many Web sites offer several different products. Each product you want to buy, you add to the "cart." Once you've loaded your cart, you "check out," which means you type in your name, address, credit card number, and all the other information the site requests and/or demands of you. When the order is complete, the customer clicks a final button to send the order.

Shopping cart software is available from many different sources on the Internet. Web hosts offer shopping carts as part of their Web packages. Type in "shopping cart" in a search engine and see what turns up. While all shopping carts are similar, there are subtle but sometimes significant differences between the carts. Some allow more flexibility and customization than others. Some are more user friendly than others.

A good shopping cart system will include an automatic follow-up e-mail sent immediately to the purchaser, confirming the order, thanking the purchaser for the order, letting the purchaser know when the goods will be shipped, and giving the purchaser a way to respond if something is wrong.

Internet buyers are quick to abandon a shopping cart that confuses them, that makes them work too hard to use the cart, or that asks too many unnecessary personal questions. Any shopping cart (or Web site) that demands personal information before the order is filled out is most likely to be abandoned.

If you want a shopping cart for your site, I suggest you visit several Web sites that have shopping carts. Go through the entire process of placing an order. Order several items, see how easy or difficult the cart is to use, how much information is demanded of you, how comfortable the process makes you feel. You can abandon the order at the last minute, after you've seen how the entire transaction proceeds.

Design your own shopping cart, or select from the different cart packages, to include the best ideas you found, and to exclude the worst.

## How The Shopping Cart Sale Works

When someone orders from your shopping cart, the order is automatically sent to you, or sent to your credit card processor, depending on who is actually processing the credit card.

Don't confuse the two steps: the shopping cart order, and the credit card payment. The shopping cart takes the order and forwards it to whoever is going to process the order. These are two separate functions.

## Secure Server

The order information the shopping cart collects from your customer travels over the Internet. This information can be read by anyone who can gain access to the information, legitimately or otherwise.

One way to protect private information from prying eyes is to use a "secure server." A secure server scrambles ("encrypts") the information into an unreadable code, so it cannot be understood until it is unscrambled. Encrypted information keeps thieves and hackers and unauthorized people from understanding the information should they be able to access it.

Most secure-server software encrypts information only while it is travelling, from your customer to you or to your credit card processor. The likelihood of someone grabbing your customer's information while it is travelling from the customer's computer to yours is highly unlikely, encrypted or not.

As soon as the information arrives, it is unencrypted. When customer information is sitting on your computer hard drive, or on your Web server's computer, it is a sitting duck for anyone trying to break into the computer. Should someone gain access to your computer or your Web server's computer, the hacker could see (and steal) your customer's information. Again, this is a very unlikely scenario.

Because secure servers encrypt information only during transmission, the protection they offer is minimal, almost worthless. But Internet shoppers don't know this. Internet shoppers think secure servers are secure. The shoppers look for the little padlock logo that tells them they are on a secure server, and they are much more likely to order from you if you have a secure server. Anything you can do to make your customers feel comfortable and safe when ordering from you, will be worth the effort.

Protect yourself from problems caused by the service that provides the shopping cart and the secure server. Find out what backup systems the provider has, what liability protection the provider offers.

## Debit Cards / Cash Cards

Debit cards (also called "cash cards" and sometimes "check cards") are processed just like credit cards. As long as the debit cards do not require a secret "pin" (personal identification number), there is no difference in how the cards are handled or the fees charged.

## Internet "Cash"

Internet services are available for people who want to shop on the Internet, but who do not have credit cards, or do not trust using their credit cards online, or are making very small purchases, usually $1 to $5.

Customers sign up with one of these "e-cash" ("digital cash") services and deposit money in an account with the service, much like putting money in a checking account at a bank. Or people authorize the service to charge their phone bill or some other account they've set up.

The merchant must also sign up with the services in order for the transaction to work. The merchant is charged a fee for each transaction, much like fees charged for credit card sales.

Because both the customer and the merchant must already be signed up with the e-cash service, very few businesses are presently using this system. But as more and more people shop on the Internet, and as more Internet businesses start charging small fees for services, we are likely to see a more user-friendly and more universal e-cash system emerge.

## Other Payment Options

Give your customers options other than online payment. Remember, many people do not trust the Internet, and they also do not trust businesses that they cannot reach other than through the Internet. Lots of people still don't have credit cards, and pay by check or money order.

Give customers a telephone number, preferably a toll-free number, where they can place an order, get information, and get help. Include a fax number for fax orders. And include a mailing address.

The more options you give your customers, the more they will trust you, and the more sales you'll make.

## Business-to-Business Sales

Most business-to-business sales on the Internet are still done the old-fashioned way, by invoice, with payment due in 30 days (or whatever terms you've agreed to). Some businesses will pay up front, with a credit card; but many want to examine the goods before paying, and many must process the paperwork through their accounting department before paying. And as you will soon learn, the bigger the business and the more sophisticated the accounting department and the computer system, the longer it takes to get paid.

Be diligent when extending credit. First of all, make sure the business is real, and is really placing an order, and not some disgruntled employee or some kid hacking away after school. Don't hesitate to telephone the company to confirm the order, maybe request a faxed confirmation. A personal connection with a business buyer, even if just over the telephone, will make all of your business dealings more likely to succeed.

Don't be afraid to talk to about payment terms, before you ship the goods or provide the services. Ask for their assurance that they will pay their bills on time. Get someone in authority to actually say, "Yes, we will pay you." Sometimes they'll say, "Well, this and that corporation extend us credit, we have an AA#1 Dun & Bradstreet rating, we are an established business, member of the Chamber of Commerce" and various and sundry impressive stuff that is of absolutely no value to you. Just repeat that all you need is their assurance you will be paid. It's a powerful "Yes" when they say it. Even crooks have a hard time going back on their word.

And then, never ship too large an order on that first order. Like the age old advice to gamblers, don't ship more than you can afford to lose.

---

# Chapter 26:
# Fraud Prevention

*"Technology facilitates pretty much anything, including parting fools from their money."*
**—Steph Marr, Vice President for Internet Security,**
**Predictive Systems, New York**

There are many steps you can take to reduce the likelihood of someone defrauding you. You can buy fraud prevention software that screens suspicious orders based on a set of criteria you enter. But if you have a small enough business where you handle all the orders personally, and if you know your business well enough to know what is usual and what is unusual, fraud prevention is not much more than common sense. In other words, if you smell a rat, be on your guard.

## Taking Orders over the Internet

Some businesses are much more vulnerable to online fraud attempts than others. Businesses selling high ticket items such as computers, cameras, and expensive jewelry, and businesses selling products people might be tempted to steal such as music CDs, are more likely to be targeted than businesses selling less expensive or less "flashy" items: books, hardware, stuff that does not attract thieves too much.

How you set up your fraud prevention depends on how your Web site is set up to handle orders. If you process your own credit card orders, you always have the opportunity to examine the orders carefully before filling them. If a credit card processor handles your orders for you, you should talk to the processor about how you can screen orders before processing them.

Get complete information from customers, including e-mail address, a phone number, and both "bill to" and "ship to" addresses if different.

Possible indications of fraudulent orders include:

1. Unusual orders, large-dollar orders, and orders for a lot of items. Most people order one item or only a few items. Someone who orders one of everything may be suspicious.

2. Orders from foreign countries.

3. Orders from free e-mail accounts such as Hotmail and Yahoo.

4. Orders with different "bill to" and "ship to" addresses.

5. Orders requesting overnight or expedited delivery. A thief won't care how much it costs to ship, since he doesn't plan to pay for it anyway.

6. Orders from unconcerned customers, such as not caring about color or size.

7. Orders that do not include the customer's phone number.

If you have a reason to be suspicious of an order, you can telephone your credit card company to verify a card member's name and address. You can also call the customer on the phone to "confirm" the order. Not many thieves will give you a valid telephone number. But use the phone confirmation as a last resort. Many people, people placing legitimate orders, may not want you calling their home or office. What if the order is a gift for someone in the family? (What if the order is a gift for someone not in the family?)

Keep in mind that credit card companies will charge your account for any fraudulent Internet orders. If the buyer doesn't pay, you the merchant are stuck, even if the card was approved. An approval is not a guarantee that the transaction is legitimate. See **Chapter 25: Online Payment Systems** for more information.

**"Now all of a sudden you're not selling a product and walking away. You're not selling inventory, you're selling a service. And with a service people have expectations. It has to be running, there has to be support, people they can talk to."**
—*Michael Ross, Publisher, World Book Inc.*

# Section Five:
# Law of the Internet

*"It's not the Wild West out there. If you couldn't do it offline, you can't do it online either."*

—Mozelle Thompson, Commissioner,
Federal Trade Commission

# Chapter 27:
# Law of the Internet

*"The regulators are still trying to figure out what they should be doing."*

**—Shari Steele, Director of Legal Services,**
**Electronic Frontier Foundation**

The Internet is no longer the untamed Wild West. The sheriff of Dodge City has arrived, governments all over the world have been putting up fences, and a new era of fence-line disputes has begun.

There is little "Internet law" as such. Most Internet activity is governed by the same laws as those in the physical world. E-commerce, however, has redefined basic ways of doing business, forcing government authorities to accommodate the new ways into the old laws. Existing business laws are being applied to the Internet, at times awkwardly, at times incorrectly, as government agencies try to fit what often looks like a square peg in a round hole. Sometimes it is as difficult as the wicked stepsisters trying to get their feet into Cinderella's shoe.

Most business laws have been around for many years, legal precedents decided, court fights long over. But with the growth of digital technology and the huge growth of the Internet and its global reach, a growing body of new laws and new interpretations of old laws is slowly accumulating. And today's "lucky" Internet businesses get to watch it in action, something modern businesses have never before had to deal with.

This Section covers all of the current and proposed laws regulating business on the Internet. But everything is in flux. Like too many software programs, the bugs aren't entirely worked out. You should keep current on new laws, and on the changes in the wind.

## Jurisdiction

Jurisdiction refers to where a transaction or an event occurs, and what government agency or what court gets to rule over the occurrence. E-commerce undermines one of the basic principles of law and taxation, which is that geography—jurisdiction—defines commercial activity.

When businesses and their customers reside in the same jurisdiction, the same city or state, problems with jurisdiction do not exist. With the Internet, more and more businesses are selling to customers in other states and other countries. If a customer wants to bring legal action against you, or you want to bring legal action against a customer, jurisdiction becomes important. Where will the case be heard? Where, for that matter, did the transaction occur?

Nobody wants to be hauled into court. But if it happens, you sure don't want to have to go to Nebraska, or Germany, to defend yourself because your small business in Oregon sold something over the Internet to someone who lives thousands of miles from you.

Some Web sites address the issue of dispute resolution, how the parties agree to handle problems, and most important, in what jurisdiction the dispute will be heard should it go to court. If you visit a site owned by an Internet Service Provider or a Credit Card Processor or other business service, somewhere hidden on the site will be a long legal contract covering disputes and jurisdiction. And in every one of those agreements, jurisdiction will be where the service is located, not where you the customer are located. When you sign up for their service, you are sure to find a statement that says something like, "By making this purchase, you agree to the service's terms and conditions. Click here to read all of the terms and conditions..." And of course, you never "click here" to read what you just agreed to. Does anybody look at these contracts?

Most small business Web sites do not include a list of terms and conditions, and most do not discuss legal jurisdiction. It's definitely not user-friendly to your customers. But it does open you up to trouble should you get in a dispute with a customer. If you don't take the initiative to establish legal ground rules, with an agreement spelled out on your Web site, some court, possibly a hostile and distant court, will do it for you.

If you want to include a "terms and conditions" agreement, have a look at some of the agreements other Web sites are forcing on their customers. Many of the agreements are "boiler plate," a standard agreement used by many different businesses. You just fill in the blanks and post it to your site.

Fortunately, the truth is that few small businesses are sued. Most problems with customers are worked out long before a lawyer is involved. It is time consuming and expensive for someone to bring a lawsuit, and few people really want to do so. But it is a risk you must weigh.


## Legal Protection

*"Congress shall make no law respecting an establishment of religion, or prohibiting the free exercise thereof; or abridging the freedom of speech, or of the press, or of the Internet, or the right of the people peaceably to assemble, and to petition the Government for a redress of grievances."*
First Amendment to the U.S. Constitution, December 15, 1791

The First Amendment of the U.S. Constitution gives you the right to put most anything you want on your Web site, other than the obvious prohibitions: Copyrighted material belonging to others. Child pornography. Libelous statements. Slander and defamation of character. Invasion of people's privacy (putting someone's photo or personal information on your Web site).

If you have something critical to put on your Web site about an individual, a group, or a business, I suggest, for starters, that you not do it. You are just asking for trouble.

If you feel you must criticize a product or a company, be sure you have solid researched proof of your charges. If you are making comparisons between your product and someone else's, be very careful that your claims can be proven. Even if you have solid proof, you are likely to be challenged, even sued, by the company you are criticizing. My advise: talk about your business and your products, don't mention the competition, and let your visitors make their own comparisons.

## Legal Liability for Your Products

Is your Web site responsible for the safety of a product you sell? Is your site responsible for the content of a book you sell? If a product you sell injures someone, if a book you sell libels someone, what problems might you encounter?

Generally speaking, the seller of a product is not held responsible for the product's safety, a book's contents, or similar problems, as long as:

1. You are not the designer or manufacturer of the product, or the author or publisher of the book.
2. You did not know there was a problem.
3. The problem was not obvious.
4. You were not negligent, such as failing to even casually examine a product before offering it for sale.
5. The product is still in its original packaging.
6. You did no assembly nor gave any advice.

Products liability insurance (covered in **Chapter 11: Insurance for Internet Businesses**) is available to protect you from lawsuits initiated by injured parties. This insurance is usually purchased by manufacturers, not sellers. But you may want to discuss the insurance with your insurance agent. The insurance may be very inexpensive, well worth the cost.

Manufacturers of products, if you ask, will often give you a statement, sometimes called a "vendors endorsement," stating that the manufacturer takes full responsibility for the manufacturer's product, and holds you harmless against all claims. A manufacturer may even indemnify you, which means the manufacturer agrees to pay any legal bills you incur fighting a product liability lawsuit.

You can put disclaimers on your products, even require the buyer to sign the disclaimer or click on a button agreeing to the disclaimer, but such disclaimers rarely hold up in court. You cannot legally make a disclaimer against your own negligence or where children are involved. And disclaimers often backfire, making customers suspicious of you, which won't help your business whatsoever.

I started this discussion with the words "generally speaking" because I want to be very clear, or maybe I should say intentionally vague, about your potential liability for what you sell.

If someone is injured by a product, that person is likely to sue everyone involved, no matter what the law says. Some laws are very specific, but many laws are written in vague terms. The laws are interpreted by judges and juries who make decisions based as much on emotion and personal prejudice as on the wording of the law. You just can't ever know 100%.

Business, by its very nature, will always have an element of risk. Being on the Internet give a business much greater exposure, and therefore a higher risk, than a small local business. But if you take reasonable precautions, if you act diligently and honestly, your chances of getting in serious trouble are very low.

# Chapter 28:
# Law by Contract

*"Treating every good idea with lawyers really points to the failure of American ingenuity in the 21st Century."*
**—John Zane, CEO, Danzhaus Co.**

Many of the dealings you will have with your Internet suppliers, Internet Service Providers, Web hosts, software manufacturers, and the companies that provide your secure payment systems, will be defined and regulated by a contract between you and the company you are doing business with. Some of your dealings with your Internet customers will also be defined by contract. Barring fraud, theft, misrepresentation, or illegal transactions, contracts usually are considered legally binding. Contracts are basically self-created laws.

Contracts go by a variety of names. Anything labeled "an agreement" is a contract. Statements with titles such as "Limitation of Liability" or "Restrictions" or "Terms and Conditions" are contracts. Guarantees and warranties are contracts.

Business dealings are more likely to be successful and free of disagreements, arguments, misunderstandings and lawsuits if they include a written contract. This is especially true for someone providing a professional service or doing a multi-faceted project. The issues of who does what, when, and for how much, can get dicey without a written contract.

A contract defines each party's responsibilities and commitments. A contract demonstrates business professionalism and weeds out insincere people. A contract will protect you from the anguish and frustration of indecisive people and people who continually change their minds and the extent of the job midstream. A contract gives both parties a sense of security. The only proof you have of the extent of your obligations is your signed agreement.

Contracts must be understandable. No whereas's, heretofore's, or legal mumbo-jumbo. Avoid words like he, she and they; it's too easy to confuse who you're talking about. Use your names, or "provider" and "client," "seller" and "buyer." Contracts should be simple and concise yet include full details. A good contract tries to answer all the questions before they're asked.

Contracts must be signed by both parties—original signatures, not faxed, not photocopied. Some contracts can be signed using digital signatures (see below).

Some clauses a contract might include:

1. The duration of the contract.
2. A description of the products or services being provided.

3. All deadlines, shipping dates, delivery times.

4. Consequences of missing the deadlines or not completing the contract.

5. Amount, terms, and timetable for payment.

6. Conditions under which the contract can be terminated.

7. If there will be out of pocket expenses, the contract should specify who pays the expenses, when and if they are to be reimbursed, and any dollar limit.

8. Limits to your liability.

9. Can any rights in the contract be sold, given or traded ("assigned") to a third party?

10. A statement that the contract cannot be verbally altered. Any changes must be in writing, signed by both parties.

Contracts don't have to be formal, legal-looking documents. Formal contracts sometimes backfire, scaring off a potential customer. A simple letter of agreement, signed by both parties, is a valid contract and may be more appropriate in many situations. Signed purchase orders are also valid contracts.

If your business is a corporation, a partnership or a limited liability company, it should be disclosed in the contract. Be sure to sign as a representative of the business (President, etc.), not as an individual, not as "owner." Make it clear that the business, not you personally, is responsible for the contract. This will help limit your personal liability.

Before you write up a contract, make a list of the things you want to cover. Take a few days, to make sure you think of everything. Look at other contracts to see how other people wrote theirs. There are books of sample contracts you can buy (or check your local library or the Internet). Trade organizations sometimes have sample contracts. Friends in business might let you have copies of their contracts (with names and numbers scratched out). Your accountant may be able to get you samples of contracts.

Contracts with designers, artists and others whose work involves intellectual property such as writing, artwork, computer programming, etc., should spell out who owns the rights to the work. Web designer contracts are covered in **Chapter 18: Web Site Design.**

Avoid oral contracts. Lawyers are fond of saying that verbal contracts are not worth the paper they're written on. Lawyers are also fond of saying that you should hire a lawyer to draft the contract. This is an expensive added cost that I feel is unnecessary. You can create a simple, basic-English contract yourself. If signed and dated by you and your designer, the contract is a valid legal document, lawyer or no lawyer.

Besides, the purpose of the contract is not to have a "legal document." The contract is not for legal protection. Legal protection has little value unless you have a lot of money to hire lawyers to wage a lawsuit. That's not why we are here. The main purpose of a contract should be to clarify an agreement, to make sure all parties fully understand the agreement, not to set up the rules for a fight. "An ounce of prevention is worth a pound of cure," Benjamin Franklin said (or Thomas Jefferson, or someone). An ounce of contract is worth *ten tons* of lawsuits.

## Other People's Contracts

If you are asked to sign someone else's contract, it's a whole different ball game. Large corporations, government agencies, landlords, banks, leasing companies, professional consultants, and independent freelancers often have their own contracts ready for you to sign, and they probably had talented and expensive lawyers create them.

Make sure you understand and fully agree with every word. Don't be too embarrassed to admit you don't know the meaning of a word. Look it up or ask. Be on your guard; nothing in these contracts is superfluous. Every clause was carefully thought out, to give the best advantage and protection to whoever had the contract prepared. And look out for the word "indemnify." It means that, if there is a lawsuit, you agree to pay the other party's legal expenses.

Just because contracts are printed on fancy paper, are formal, technical, legal, and etc., they are not cemented in stone—until you sign them. There is no such thing as a "standard" contract. A contract, remember, is an agreement. Both parties agree to something, and the contract commits that agreement to writing. If you don't agree with what is in the contract, do not sign the contract. You can take out your pen and change any contract, eliminate or rewrite sections and conditions you don't agree to.

## Online Contracts

Most small businesses have no real need for a contract with online customers. But if you are providing an Internet service, or a financial service, an online contract will define the limits of your responsibilities and liabilities. Quite often, when you make a purchase on a Web site, somewhere on the site is a list of legal disclaimers that say something like, "By making this purchase, you agree to the terms and conditions of this contract. Click here to read the terms and conditions." Do you want or need such a contract on your site? Not likely.

But if you are buying a product or service from a Web site that has one of these contracts, you ought to take the time to read through it. Make sure you are agreeing to what you think you are agreeing to.

## A Warning

I don't guarantee that the contract details in this chapter will make your contract legally binding. Your state may have contract laws and filing requirements, may require some precise legal wording, a witness or notarization. If a lot is at stake in a contract, have it examined by a lawyer. The purpose of a contract is to avoid legal entanglements. Once a contract winds up in court, everybody loses.

## Digital Signatures

Contracts are not legally binding unless the contracts are signed by all parties to the transaction. Purchase orders, sales agreements, work orders, projects, loans, insurance papers, tax forms, even letters are legally binding when signed. It is difficult to force compliance, or prove that an agreement was reached, if the documents are not signed. Even businesses that know their customers and have excellent relationships with their customers usually get all sales and purchase agreements in writing, signed, as a standard procedure.

A federal law, The Electronic Signatures in Global and National Commerce Act (sometimes called the Digital Signatures Act or the E-Signature Act), allows contracts to be signed over the Internet by what is called a digital signature, electronic signature, or e-signature. All three terms mean the same thing. An e-signature can significantly cut down the time it takes to process an online transaction.

The federal E-Signature Act applies only to documents involving interstate commerce. Contracts between two parties in the same state do not come under this law. But many states have adopted a law called the Uniform Electronic Transactions Act (UETA), or some modified version of the UETA, for in-state transactions.

Under both the federal law and the UETA, both parties to an electronic contract must mutually agree, in advance, to use and recognize electronic signatures. This agreement must be explicitly stated and included in e-signed documents. Specifically excluded from the E-Signature law are legal personal and family documents such as divorce, wills, evictions, and foreclosures.

An electronic signature can take many forms. The law does not define exactly what an e-signature is. An e-signature could resemble a real signature, it could be a password, it could be a series of coded numbers, it could be a "click-here" button on your computer screen. The law does not state how digital signatures should look, nor how they should be verified or authenticated. The law does not endorse a specific technology. As the law reads, you can put your name on an e-mail, state that it is your official digital signature, and thereby create a legal document. The law does not mandate loss protection and does not provide remedies for losses.

There are simple digital-signature programs, and what are called "digital certificates," that let users create and issue their own coded e-signatures, though with minimum security.

For important and high-dollar business dealings, if you are going to sign a contract with a digital signature, a much higher level of security is necessary. The other party needs some way of knowing that it is really you signing the contract. You need to know that it is really the other party receiving the documents you are sending over the Internet. And both of you need to know that the documents are not being altered in transit.

The process of signing and transmitting digitally-signed documents, where there are substantial protections against error and fraud, requires special software, elaborate passwords, and third-party intermediaries, called Internet Trust Providers, who route the transaction, encode the documents, and guarantee that the signers are legitimate. The Internet Trust Provider issues you a unique digital signature. Then any time you want to use that signature, the other party to the contract can check in with the Internet Trust Provider to make sure that you and your signature match.

Right now, several different Internet services are experimenting with different technologies to make digital signatures work. In a few years, there likely will be a uniform standard used by everyone, and a few trusted providers, most likely large financial institutions, banks or possibly the credit card companies. However, the digital certification providers are likely to apply disclaimers, which would dramatically reduce the value of the service they offer.

All the technological advances in the world may never adequately substitute for a handshake, for looking someone in the eye when making a deal, for having a person pick up a pen and sign his or her name.

The federal e-signatures law states that no one can be required to use or accept electronic signatures or records. At this early stage of development, that may be an excellent course.

# Chapter 29:
# Taxes

*"We're in a new economy. The times have changed greatly. Our tax system has not."*

**—Jesse Ventura, Governor, Minnesota**

## The "Tax Free" Internet

Disregard all the magazine and newspaper articles and television stories and double-talking politicians. The Internet is not tax free. Internet businesses are subject to the exact same tax laws as all other businesses.

The federal Internet Tax Freedom Act, the one everyone waves like a banner at the Boston Tea Party, really accomplished very little. The Act states that no state nor the federal government can levy any new tax on Internet businesses or on Internet access. The key word is "new." Any taxes enacted before the Act came along are still in place. That includes sales tax, income tax, and all the licenses and permits that governments have been levying since 1775, when Patrick Henry told the First Continental Congress, "Give me my permits or give me death."

The only taxes the Internet Tax Freedom Act actually nipped in the bud were new taxes on Internet access charges, what you pay your ISP or Web host.

The Internet Tax Freedom Act was passed after a few states had already levied a tax on Internet access charges. Some of those states still tax Internet access.

The Internet Tax Freedom Act is scheduled to expire in October, 2001. Congress will most likely extend the Act, probably for several years.

## Sales Tax on Internet Businesses

Internet sales are subject to the exact same sales tax laws that apply to businesses not on the Internet.

Sales tax laws are state laws. There is no federal sales tax. Most, but not all states have a sales tax. States, counties and cities may all have a sales tax, but usually it is reported on one combined sales tax return.

State sales tax laws apply to all businesses with a physical presence in that state. Sales tax laws are based on a legal concept known as "nexus," physical presence.

If you have a physical presence in a state, you are subject to that state's sales tax laws, you collect sales tax on taxable sales made in that state. If you have no physical presence in a state, you are not subject to that state's sales tax laws, and you do not collect sales tax for sales made to residents of that state.

Before the Internet came along, physical presence (nexus) meant an office, store, or warehouse in a state, or travelling sales people in the state. With the growth of the Internet, states are trying to redefine nexus, trying to legally define when an Internet site has a physical presence in a given state.

The fact that your Web site can be viewed and downloaded by someone in another state does not create nexus. You have no physical presence in a state just because someone in that state can access your Web site.

However, a few states claim that if your Web server (your Web host) is in their state, you have a physical presence in that state, and therefore subject to that state's sales tax laws, even though your business is located entirely in another state. The state's logic is that your Web site is located on a Web server, so your Web site is located in whatever state your Web sever is in, giving your business a "physical presence" in that state.

This legal interpretation obviously stretches "physical presence" well beyond how most people would define it and would probably be overruled if someone eventually challenged it in court. But you don't want to be the guinea pig who gets to go to court, and you don't need to be hassled by some state, two thousand miles from you, desperate to collect sales tax anyway it can.

Find out where your Web server is based, and find out if the Web server's state is trying to collect sales tax from the Web server's clients. Log onto the Web server's state Web site (**www.state.[state's two-letter abbreviation].us**) and see if there are any sales tax rules posted. Discuss this problem with the Web server; call the state's sales tax office on the phone to get some advice (and if you do, ask them to mail you a copy of the published laws, so you can verify what you were told).

Fortunately, most states do not consider a Web server as a physical presence. Most states view Web servers as a form of electronic forwarding agent, completely separate from your business. Even in the few states that want to tax you if your Web server is in their state, the likelihood that the state will come after your small business is about zero. To my knowledge, it has never happened. I think the states are making a lot of noise, because they are frustrated and very angry over lost sales tax revenue. Macbeth recognized it four hundred years ago: "Sound and fury, signifying nothing."

## More "Nexus" Issues

Another nexus problem involves Web businesses that contract with other businesses to warehouse and ship products, to accept returns, or to do repairs. For example, let's say you have a business in Minnesota, selling porch swings over the Internet. But you don't keep swings in stock at your business. The swings are in your distributor's warehouse in Louisiana, and are shipped from your distributor directly to your customer. If your customer is in Minnesota, your own state, you must collect sales tax. But if your customer is in Louisiana, the state where your distributor is based, must you collect Louisiana sales tax? This shipping arrangement is known as "drop shipping," and most states have specific rules about the taxability of drop shipped goods. This is a different situation than having your own warehouse, which clearly is a physical presence, and subject to the state's sales tax laws.

Some large corporations, those with stores in several states, have come up with an ingenuous (actually, disingenuous) way to avoid collecting sales tax on Internet sales. These clever businesses set up separate corporations just to run their Internet operations. These businesses are locating their Internet-only subsidiaries in tax-free states, to avoid collecting sales tax on Internet transactions. The corporations and their lawyers claim that the Internet corporation is separate from the corporation that owns the stores, and that the Internet corporation has no stores, so it has no physical presence in any state except the one where the corporate offices and warehouses are located. The corporations claim to have found a legal loophole to get out of sales tax obligations. The affected states quite obviously smell a rat, and are challenging the businesses in court.

## General Sales Tax Rules

Basic sales tax laws are the same for all states, for all businesses: In-state sales, sales to customers in your own state, are subject to your state's sales tax laws. Out-of-state sales are exempt from sales tax. Beyond this basic law, sales tax laws vary greatly from state to state.

Generally, retail goods (goods sold to the public; and goods sold to businesses for their own use, not for resale or manufacture) are subject to sales tax. But every state is different. Some states tax food but not clothing. Some states tax clothing but not newspapers. The list of what is and isn't taxable goes on like an endless run of sausages.

In all states, wholesale goods are exempt from sales tax. Wholesale refers to goods that are sold by one business to another, to re-sell or to go into a manufactured product. Don't confuse "wholesale" with "discount." The ads in the papers that say "Wholesale to the Public," "Whole-sale—Factory To You," or some other misuse of the word are actually referring to discount retail sales, subject to sales tax.

Services (as opposed to products) are taxed in a few states, not taxed in others. The legal definitions of "products" and "services" must be carefully understood. Different states have different definitions of what is a taxable product and what is a non-taxable service. Is a custom designed logo, or Web page, or software a product, or a service? Your state's sales tax department will have written rules spelling out what is and isn't taxable.

Every business subject to the sales tax must have a Sales Tax Permit, also known as a Sellers Permit, or a Resale License. You do not need a sales tax permit from any state expect your own, unless you have "nexus" in another state (as explained above). Sales tax permits are covered in **Chapter 10: Permits and Licenses.**

## Sales Tax on Downloaded Products

Books, reports, software, music, and other data that people purchase over the Internet, and download to their own computers (as opposed to purchasing a physical product that is mailed or handed to the customer) are subject to sales tax in some states but not in others.

Many states do not tax anything downloaded from the Internet. Some states tax what they call "information services" or "computer services" and include anything downloaded in this definition. Some states consider downloaded information to be a product, subject to sales tax. Some states tax downloaded software but not other downloaded "products." And states that do not now apply sales tax to anything downloaded may well try to redefine downloaded data as a tangible product, subject to sales tax. States are looking every which way for sales tax revenue. The logic the states use is often vague and arbitrary, but that really is not the issue. If your state taxes downloaded data, then you must collect the sales tax.

If you charge your Internet customers to download anything from your site, contact your state's sales tax department and find out if your state taxes downloaded information. And be specific about what you are selling: some states tax specific downloaded purchases but not others.

Also investigate the state your Web server is in. Some states consider the Web server to be the supplier of downloaded information. People "pick up" the download at the server's location, not at your location. If your Web server is in a state that taxes downloaded information, will you be required to collect sales tax in that state?

Keep in mind, this is an issue only for sales to customers who reside in your own state (or possibly to customers who live in the same state as your Web server). What is interesting here is that you may not know where your customers reside. An online sale can be completed without getting your customer's address, since you are not mailing anything to the customer, and his e-mail address of YoBaby@hotmail.com isn't much help. So on your Web site, you inform your customers that if they are in your state, you must charge sales tax. And every single customer says, ah, no, I'm not in your state. You've done what you can do.

## Use Tax

Technically, *all* online purchases are subject to sales tax. The out-of-state sales tax exemptions explained above apply only to the seller. The seller is not required to collect sales tax from out of state customers.

But when a buyer purchases goods from an out-of-state seller, the buyer is required to pay tax on those goods. The tax is called a "use tax," and every state that has a sales tax also has a use tax. The difference? Sales tax is collected by the seller. Use tax is paid directly by the buyer, and remitted to the buyer's state.

Never heard of the use tax? Never paid a use tax? Don't know anyone who has ever paid use tax? Well, that's the problem the states are wrestling with. Very few people know the use tax exists, and almost no one pays it.

In some states, state income tax returns have a box where people compute the use tax on merchandise they purchased from out-of-state vendors, and remit the tax along with their state income tax return.

Sellers have no legal obligation to notify their customers that the customers are supposed to pay use tax on their purchases.

## The Sales Tax Wars

You should keep a close watch on the interstate sales tax problem. It will not go away. The current debate—what is "nexus," what companies are taxable by what government jurisdictions—misses the point. Local governments need to collect tax money, and sales tax is a major part of state and local government budgets. States often use sales tax to fund schools. Local communities depend on sales tax for basic services such as fire and police protection and street maintenance.

Loss of sales tax has always been a problem with catalog and mail order sales. But with the growth of the Internet, the loss of sales tax revenue is reaching levels that are starting to worry state and local governments across the country.

This is also a problem for local businesses that must collect sales tax. If an Internet business can lure a customer away from a local business by not charging sales tax, the local business and the local economy suffer.

The sales tax issue is a hotly debated one. As Internet commerce grows, as large Internet businesses devise more clever ways to avoid collecting sales taxes often on legal technicalities, and as more local Main Street businesses complain of a loss of sales to tax-free Internet businesses, a more equitable, nationwide sales tax law will most likely emerge, something this country has never seen before.

Already, 38 states have gotten together and ratified with they call the "Streamlined Sales Tax Project." This Project is a proposal, not yet law by any means, but it may give you an idea of things to come. The states participating in the Project have agreed to adopt a uniform model as to what types of products,  and what services if any, would be taxable. The states would have flexibility in determining what rate of sales tax to charge. The state of Pennsylvania, for example, might charge a 6% sales tax on all goods deemed taxable, while Oregon might charge 3% on the same goods. Your business would be required to collect 6% from Pennsylvania residents and 3% from Oregon residents. Whether you would have to file fifty different sales tax returns, or one giant sales tax return for all fifty states, has not been worked out. If this sounds like a nightmare of paperwork, I would agree. Possibly Congress will step in with an alternative proposal for a national sales tax that requires one sales tax rate and one return. Keep your eyes on this one.

## Income Tax

The income tax laws for Internet businesses are identical to the laws for all other businesses.

If you are a sole proprietor, you must file a federal income tax return if your *net* earnings from self-employment (your business *net* profit) is $400 or more. Business income minus expenses equals *net* profit. If your business is a partnership, corporation, or Limited Liability Company (an LLC), you must file an income tax return no matter what the profit or loss is. Legal structures for businesses are covered in **Chapter 7: Legal Structure for Your Internet Business**.

Self-employed professionals, freelancers, consultants, free agents, independent contractors, designers, and other people working for themselves often do not consider themselves to be running a business. But the IRS makes no distinction between businesses that call themselves "businesses," and individuals who give themselves other titles. If you are self-employed—that is not on someone else's payroll, with payroll deductions and W-2 statements at the end of the year—the IRS considers you to be a sole proprietor. The tax laws are the same for you as for every other sole proprietor.

## Income Tax Basics

Most everything you do in starting and operating an Internet business is common sense, not difficult to understand. The rules of business, after all, were made by people wanting to sell something and people wanting to buy something. Even bookkeeping is not complicated. Adding and subtracting, mostly.

But income taxes...Income tax laws were created by politicians. And like many politicians, income tax laws don't always make sense and don't always accomplish what they claim to accomplish.

Almost every business will benefit from hiring a tax accountant to prepare income tax returns. But even with the best accountant, every business owner should have a general understanding of income tax laws, what must be reported, what can and what cannot be deducted.

There are three parts to a business income tax return: income; cost of goods sold; and expenses.

**1. Income.** Income is what your customers, clients, or patients pay you for your goods or services, what the IRS calls "gross receipts." Income does not include any of your own money you put into your business, any loans you receive, or any money from investors or partners.

The income is first reduced by "returns and allowances," which are any refunds or credits you make to your customers. Income is then further reduced by something called "cost of goods sold."

**2. Cost of Goods Sold.** Cost of goods sold is a very important tax law to understand. When a business buys goods to resell, or parts for repair work, or materials to use in crafts or in manufacturing, the business cannot write off the cost of this inventory until the inventory is sold. There are several exceptions to this law, ways to write off damaged goods or goods whose value has declined, but generally, any inventory on hand at the end of the year cannot be deducted on your income taxes this year—even though you had to spend your money, possibly a lot of money, to buy the inventory. The year you sell the inventory is the year you get the tax deduction. If you business is a service business, no goods for sale, no parts, you have no cost of goods sold, one less tax nuisance to deal with; you can skip down to the third part, Expenses. Cost of goods sold is calculated as follows:

1. From your expenditure ledger, get the total figure for inventory purchases for the year.

2. At December 31, you list all the inventory still on hand, and calculate the cost. This is called "taking a physical inventory." The word "inventory" is used both as a noun, the goods themselves, and a verb, the act of counting and valuing the goods. If the inventory on hand at year end is unsalable, damaged, worthless, or worth less than what you paid for it, value the year-end inventory not at its cost, but at its market value, what you can sell it for.

3. Purchases during the year (1) less inventory still on hand at the end of the year (2) equals your cost of goods sold.

In future years, start with the inventory on hand at the end of the prior year (computed under #2 above), add purchases for the year, and then subtract inventory on hand at the end of the new year.

**3. Expenses.** Income ("gross receipts") less returns and allowances, less cost of goods sold, give you what the IRS calls "gross income." Gross income is then reduced by all the deductible expenses the IRS will let you write off. The IRS lists only about twenty expenses on the tax return, but there are hundreds of expenses that businesses can legitimately deduct. My book **422 Tax Deductions for Businesses and Self Employed Individuals** (Bell Springs Publishing, 800-515-8050) lists every one of them (I think).

Generally, if an expense is a legitimate business expense (what the IRS calls "ordinary and necessary"), if the amount is reasonable ("not lavish or extravagant under the circumstances"), and if the expense is not specifically prohibited by law, it is deductible. Some of the larger and more important tax deductions, and some of the lesser known tax deductions, for Internet businesses are:

**Start Up Costs.** This is an important area of tax law for new businesses. The expenses you incur before you actually "open for business" and start earning money are called "start up costs" (though they are really pre-start-up costs). Some start up costs are deductible and some are not. Before you spend a lot of money you may not be able to deduct, talk to an accountant. Or better yet, start your business on a shoestring, put off as many expenses as possible until after the business is operating.

**Business Assets.** Equipment, tools, furniture, machinery, and vehicles can be written off the year of purchase. The maximum write off in any one year is $24,000, all assets combined. Any purchases in excess of $24,000 must be depreciated, a tax term that means the cost is written off over several years. I simplify the law here: There are many rules and restrictions to this deduction.

**Wages.** All employee wages are 100% deductible. This includes family members on your payroll. The deduction does not include payments to the owner of the business, unless the business is a corporation. This is explained in **Chapter 7: Legal Structure**.

**Taxes.** Business-related taxes are deductible, with the exception of federal income tax and self-employment tax. State income taxes are deductible on your federal tax return.

**Health Insurance.** Sole proprietors, partners in partnerships, members of limited liability companies, and owners of S corporations can deduct 60% of the cost of health insurance for themselves, their spouses and dependents. Owner-employees of C corporations can deduct 100% of the cost of health insurance. Employers can deduct 100% of the cost of the health insurance for their employees.

**Travel.** Legitimate business travel is deductible. Meals and entertainment are only 50% deductible, but transportation, lodging, and incidental expenses are 100% deductible. IRS travel rules are very specific, and the IRS is very suspicious of business travel deductions. The IRS thinks that too many of us entrepreneurial types are taking vacations and writing them off as a business expense. If you have travel expenses, make sure they are well documented.

**Education Expenses.** The cost of education for any self-employed individual is deductible, if the education maintains or improves a skill required in your business. Education expenses are not allowed if the education is required to meet minimum educational requirements of your present business or if the education will qualify you for a new trade or business. Employers are allowed a deduction for job-related education expenses paid for their employees.

**Retirement Accounts.** Business owners can set up several different tax-deductible retirement accounts for themselves—called IRAs, SEPs, Keoghs, and SIMPLE Plans—and postpone paying income taxes on the profits deposited into the retirement accounts. The rules vary greatly from one account to the next. Employers can set up retirement accounts for their employees, and get a 100% tax deduction.

**Prepayments.** Some prepayments are deductible the year you make the payment, and some are not deductible until the year the payment applies to.

**Tax Credits.** Tax credits are special tax incentives created by Congress, to stimulate the economy or to encourage businesses to act in socially or environmentally responsible ways. Tax credits are not tax-deductible expenses, because they do not reduce your business profit. Tax credits reduce your taxes directly, dollar for dollar. Tax credits are a little gold mine, they are. Tax credits come and go, available one year and not the next. Current tax credits are listed on the IRS's Web site **www.irs.gov**.

**Home Businesses.** Home businesses have some tax deduction laws only for home businesses. They are covered in **Chapter 42: Income Tax Laws for Home Businesses**.

## Estimated Taxes

Not only does the IRS want you to pay income taxes, the IRS wants you to pay them in advance. If your federal tax for the current year, income and self-employment combined, is estimated to be $1,000 or more ($500 for corporations), you are required to pay the tax in quarterly installments. The four installments are due April 15, June 15, September 15, and the following January 15. Estimated are filed on Form 1040-ES.

How do you estimate your taxes? You can base your estimate on your prior year's taxes, even if you were not in business then. Whatever your total tax came to last year, divide it by four and send the IRS four equal installments. If your total federal tax last year, income and self employment tax combined, was less than $1,000, you are not required to make any estimated tax payments.

There is a lot of fine print to the estimated tax requirements. (Of course. If the IRS wrote instructions how to boil water, there'd be a lot of fine print). Read all about it on the IRS web site **www.irs.gov**.

## Tax Assistance on the Internet

When you have an income tax question, the first place to look on the Internet is the Internal Revenue Service's Web site **www.irs.gov**.

The IRS's Web site has a "FAQ" (frequently asked questions) page. The site also has online versions of the 50 or more publications the IRS puts out and updates every year, on just about every tax subject imaginable. The publications are detailed and complete, and even readable. But the laws are often convoluted, a fault of Congress not the IRS. The IRS's admirable attempt to translate poorly-written laws into English can make for confusing reading. They are confusing laws.

You will not always find what you are looking for on the IRS's Web site. There are many other sites on the Internet that discuss, interpret, and analyze tax laws. Typing in a few pertinent words in a search engine will provide a list of sites that will keep you surfing until long after dinner is cold and everybody else has gone to bed.

A few tax information sites are owned by legal publishers, who want you to buy their publications or pay money to log onto their sites. Sometimes they will have brief, partial answers to your questions on the free portion of their site, but their goal is to sell you the full information. Many tax information sites are free newsletters published by accounting firms and legal firms. These sites are primarily meant to be a calling card. If you like the newsletter, maybe you will hire the firm.

Like many Internet searches, trying to get specific tax information is a time consuming and sometimes frustrating process, requiring you to weed out superfluous, inapplicable, incorrect, and out of date information.

Out of date tax information is the most problematic. On many tax Web site, the tax information is sometimes several years old. A law that passed two or three years ago may have gone through several revisions since the Web site posted the information. Even on the IRS Web site, the tax information often applies to the previous year. A tax law that applies to last year could be quite different than the law that applies to this year. Always check the date the information was posted, determine what year the laws apply to.

Many tax-information Web sites are state sites, covering state tax laws, not federal laws. Be careful not to read some Massachusetts or Wyoming law by mistake.

Steer clear of Web sites sponsored by tax protest groups and by people who guarantee that they can cut your taxes to zero.

## Filing Tax Returns on the Internet

The IRS and many states allow you to file tax returns over the Internet. Sales tax, payroll, excise taxes, and other tax returns can often be filed easily and quickly, depending on how complex your reporting requirements are, how familiar you are with the reporting requirements, and how well designed the government Web sites are. Many online tax returns are simple fill-in-the-blanks forms, just about foolproof.

Income taxes, however, are a different breed of cat. Most businesses will not be able to file their income taxes online. Business income tax returns, even for very small businesses, are often too complex to do over the Internet. Many forms are not available for online filing. And many of your tax options are not fully explained. What's more, if you pay your income taxes online with a credit card, the credit card companies charge a processing fee for income tax payments. This is in addition to any finance charges you may incur.

Unless you have a very simple business, I suggest you hire a tax accountant to help you with your tax return. There is just too much to know. It is too easy to make a mistake, one likely to result in more taxes than you legally have to pay, and one likely to invite an unnecessary IRS audit. Income tax software, which has to be rewritten every year for new tax laws, often has bugs and problems with complex business tax issues.

The business owner is the ultimate do-it-yourself kind of person. But this is one area where it is more than worth your time, peace of mind, and money, to hire a professional.

## Maintaining Tax Records

Many taxpayers maintain electronic records, which is okay with the IRS as long as the records are available to the IRS if you are audited. In the event of an audit, you can ask the IRS what formats are acceptable: CD, floppy disk, online (accessed by a temporary password), or paper.

---

# Chapter 30:
# Laws and Regulations

*"Never assume what you're doing is legal."*
—**Rodney Cobb, Staff Attorney, American Planning Association**

## Restricted Sales

Many states forbid, restrict, or license Internet sales of alcoholic beverages, tobacco products, firearms, and vehicles. These restrictions apply to all Internet businesses, regardless of where the businesses are located. If you plan to sell any of these restricted products over the Internet, you must investigate the laws in every state where your customer's reside.

## Alcohol Sales

All states regulate the sale of alcoholic beverages within their boundaries. Many states have extended these laws to the Internet, prohibiting out-of-state businesses from selling alcohol directly to in-state residents.

Seven states make it a felony. In some states it is even illegal for an in-state alcohol retailer or winery to sell and ship directly to an in-state consumer.

There are presently a string of lawsuits, brought mostly by small wineries, trying to overturn the state Internet sales laws. There are over two thousand small wineries in the United States, most family owned, and most with poor distribution. Opening up the Internet to sales will help every one of these small businesses tremendously.

States, and in-state alcohol distributors and wholesalers, are vigorously fighting the lawsuits. States are very protective of their rights, and even more protective of their in-state businesses, particularly their large in-state businesses, such as alcohol wholesalers.

States have a long history of legal precedent in their favor. The 21st Amendment to the U.S. Constitution gives states full power to regulate alcohol sales. There is even a new federal law that specifically addresses interstate sales, making it very clear that states can prohibit alcohol sales from out-of-state marketers.

Some states do allow small shipments to in-state consumers. Some states only allow Internet sales of private-label brands, and only those brands that are not available in any stores or restaurants in their state. Some states charge a licensing fee to wineries and other alcohol retailers before the states will let the retailers sell to consumers in their state.

In most states, out-of-state producers of alcoholic beverages can sell to in-state distributors, that is, sell to wholesalers. Some states allow you to sell to in-state retailers, yet some states even prohibit these sales, requiring all alcohol sales to go through distributor middlemen.

If your business plans to market alcohol over the Internet, you must research each state's laws to determine who you can and cannot ship to. You may want to log onto some Web sites maintained by small wineries, and see how they are handling sales. Log onto **www.wineinstitute.org**, the Web site for a trade organization of wineries. The site lists regulations for all fifty states regarding sales of wine.

States that do allow Internet alcohol sales demand that sellers comply with age verification requirements, sometimes difficult on the anonymous Internet. Alcohol retailers on the Internet have a warning on their Web sites prohibiting purchases by underage individuals. About as effective as a "Stay Off The Grass" sign in City Park. Purchasers must type in their birth date and affirm that they are not making it up. Since nobody ever gives phony birth dates to Internet companies, that solves that problem, right? Finally, when the booze is delivered, a person at least 21 years of age must sign for it and present an ID. However, delivery drivers, with five hundred packages to deliver by 5 pm, do not always ask for IDs.

Still, how many teenagers are going onto the Internet, selecting a fine Cabernet from booze.com, giving a valid credit card number and home address, and waiting every day for the UPS driver to show up, hoping their parents aren't home?

The issue, of course, has nothing to do with kids buying booze over the Internet. That's just a smoke screen. This is a turf war, established industries protecting their territory. The Internet is the biggest threat to established ways of doing business since, well, since they were established. The old guard isn't going to give up without a fight. And if they can get their state to back them up with restrictive state laws, what else do you expect?

Shipments of alcoholic beverages must be done through United Parcel Service, FedEx or another commercial carrier. It is against the law to ship any alcoholic beverages through the U.S. Postal Service.

## Tobacco, Firearms, and Vehicles

(No, this chapter is not about having some fun in the backwoods in Alabama, folks, we're discussing state laws.)

Some states restrict the sale of cigarettes and other tobacco products over the Internet. Internet businesses that plan to sell tobacco products should research each state's laws.

A few states restrict the sale of firearms over the Internet. Some members of Congress are trying to pass a federal law requiring online gun sellers to be licensed gun dealers, requiring background checks and waiting periods.

Some states restrict vehicle sales over the Internet.

## Privacy

Privacy, or more to the point the invasion of privacy, is a problem on the Internet. People are aware that if they give out personal information to Internet sites, those sites can use that information however they want, and can sell that information to other Web sites or anybody they choose. People are aware that many Web sites put "cookies" (downloaded information "trackers") on their hard drives, without their permission or knowledge. These cookies can snoop around your computer and can send information about you back to the Web site that launched the cookie.

People resent this intrusion, and they fear that information about them will wind up in the hands of credit card thieves, or captured by snooping Web sites gathering personal, financial or medical data without their permission, or at Web sites they find offensive or embarrassing.

Privacy is, at this point, an ambiguous legal area. There are presently two federal laws affecting privacy on the Internet.

The Federal Trade Commission's Children's Online Privacy Protection Act (COPPA) prohibits collecting personal information from children under the age of thirteen without their parent's permission. Web sites must obtain verifiable parent consent before asking children for their names, addresses, phone numbers or any other information that can be used to identify the child. As of this writing, COPPA is being challenged in the U.S. Supreme Court.

A law called the Financial Services Modernization Act, also called the Gramm-Leach-Bliley Act, requires financial institutions to get a customer's permission before sharing the customer's personal information with other businesses. The Act also requires the financial institutions to have secure Web sites, conduct risk assessments, and protect their information from "threats, hazards, and unauthorized access." Although this act was aimed at banks and other financial organizations, the act does not define with a "financial institution" is. The definition might be very narrow, or might include any business offering financing to customers. So far, no specific regulations or court cases have defined the limits of this act.

There are no other federal laws protecting privacy on the Internet. But every year, one or two bills are introduced in Congress attempting to put legal restrictions on the use of personal information. Many states are also considering such legislation. It is inevitable that Congress will eventually pass laws restricting the use of personal information on the Net.

The U.S. Federal Trade Commission, the government agency responsible for consumer protection laws, false advertising laws, and eventually (most likely) online privacy laws, urges Web sites to (1) provide notice to visitors as to the information being gathered and how it will be used; (2) allow visitors to choose what information you may gather and what you may do with it; (3) provide visitors access to review and correct their data; and (4) develop security measures to protect the data from unauthorized use. These FTC "urgings" do not carry the weight of law, yet. But they are a good indication where the FTC is most likely headed, when they finally have legal authority to make and enforce Internet privacy rules.

Even without legal requirements, you may want to address the issue of privacy on your Web site, making it very clear to your site's visitors that (1) you do or do not gather information about them; (2) you do or do not make that information available to others; (3) you do or do not send out cookies to invade their computers. I think your customers—and prospective customers—will appreciate and trust you more for addressing the issues up front.

Although you are not required to post a privacy policy on your Web site, once your policies are on your Web site for all to see, you are legally obligated to uphold them. Written privacy policies are considered contracts, and are legally binding.

If you have a privacy policy that you think your visitors and customers will like, a policy that promises maximum privacy for your visitors, make your policy part of your marketing. Display it prominently on your home page, mention it in e-mails and advertising.

My own publisher, Bell Springs Publishing, posts this very simple policy on its web site: "We respect your privacy. We do not sell, rent, or trade your name to any other business. We do not send unsolicited advertisements. You will not be added to any spam or junk mail lists."

## Protecting Customer Information

Some states have laws requiring businesses to take specific steps to protect customer records. With or without laws, however, every business should take every reasonable precaution to keep customers' personal and financial information safe.

Keep credit card numbers and other personal data in a secure area. If the information is on paper, lock the file cabinets. If the information is on your computer, limit access to the information. Delete customer information from your computer as soon as you no longer need it. Destroy old and unneeded customer records, especially if they are sensitive.

Many Web sites keep their customers' personal information on the Web site, so when a customer returns to the site to reorder something, the customer does not have to re-enter all the information. While this is a time-saving benefit to customers, it also is a potential problem. Should a hacker, or a disgruntled employee, gain access to the site, he gains access to every customer's personal information. Every time you hear on the news about online credit card theft, the credit card numbers that were stolen were stored on some business's Web site.

Many businesses retain a file of customer names and addresses, but do not retain credit card numbers more than a month or so after a purchase. When a customer reorders, the businesses must get the customer's credit card numbers a second time, which is more work, but provides a measure of security for you and your customers.

If you have customers who return regularly to your site, to place repeat online orders, you will have to weigh the benefits and the risks of storing customer information online.

## Spam

"Spam" is the common term for unsolicited junk e-mail. Named after the Hormel meat product in a can, electronic spam is universally hated. Internet service providers try to keep "spammers" (people who send spam) off their servers, and many ISPs offer to block spam sent to their customers.

Several states have enacted laws restricting spam, but there are no federal laws, yet. A federal bill called the Unsolicited Electronic Mail Act is working its way through Congress, and may become law in the near future. There is already a law prohibiting unsolicited faxes, so a law aimed at identifying, reducing, or totally eliminating spam seems likely to pass.

## Disabled Access to Your Web Site

At present, the federal government does not require businesses to make their Web sites accessible to handicapped people. But there are two federal laws that address handicapped access, and one or both may eventually require commercial Web sites to be designed to allow handicapped access.

## Americans With Disabilities Act

Businesses that are open to the public must comply with the Americans With Disabilities Act (ADA). The Act requires that, "All public accommodations must provide reasonable access to persons with disabilities." Who comes under the classification "persons with disabilities" is argued in the courts regularly.

Until recently, "public accommodations" referred to retail stores, restaurants, movie theaters, amusement parks, shopping centers, and other physical business locations open to the public. "Reasonable access" referred primarily to wheelchair access.

Web sites must give some thought to the Americans With Disabilities Act. Disabled organizations are arguing that the ADA applies to the Internet. The organizations want commercial Web sites to be accessible to blind users, and to those who cannot manipulate a mouse.

The U.S. Department of Justice ruled, several years ago, that Web sites are public accommodations and must therefore offer access to the disabled. The government, however, has not yet acted on this ruling.

How Web sites are expected to comply with the ADA, and whether the government will start enforcing the ADA on the Internet, is not known.

## The "Section 508" Rule

A law called the Federal Information Technology Accessibility Initiative, better known as the "Section 508" rule (a new section added to the Federal Rehabilitation Act), will soon require that all federal government Web sites be accessible by disabled people.

But here's the wrinkle: Section 508 may eventually apply to businesses contracting with the federal government. If you sell to the U.S. government, you may be required to design your Web site so it has disabled access. The U.S. government has said that Section 508 applies only to government Web sites, but people who have studied Section 508 feel that it may in fact be extended to government contractors.

If you sell to the federal government, keep an eye on this legislation.

## Making Your Site Handicapped-Friendly

Handicapped people are on the Internet, and they are all looking for Web sites they can access. There is software that can be built into your Web site that allows blind people to read Web pages.

Rather than waiting for some law to force you to redesign your Web site, you may want to look into doing it now, and welcoming a whole new group of potential customers to your site.

## Consumer Protection Laws

The Federal Trade Commission (the FTC) has regulated advertising, guarantees and other consumer issues for many years. The FTC has been looking long and hard at the Internet, and is starting to crack down on fraudulent and deceptive advertising claims being made by Internet businesses.

All Federal Trade Commission consumer-protection laws apply to the Internet. The FTC has issued a statement that all FTC rules and guidelines that use the words "written," "writing," and "printed" will apply online.

Some of the basic FTC requirements every Internet business must comply with:

**Guarantees and Warranties.** A warranty refers to the product itself: it will perform as promised for a given period of time. Warranties must be made available to customers before they buy.

A guarantee is a promise of customer satisfaction: the customer can get an exchange or refund even if the product lives up to its warranty. You are legally required to honor any guarantee you make. Statements such as "Satisfaction Guaranteed" and "Lifetime Guarantee" and "Money Back Guarantee" must be carefully worded, as to exactly what rights your customers do and do not have.

**Shipping Delays.** Internet businesses are also mail order businesses, and they must comply with the Mail Order Merchandise Rule: Sellers must ship merchandise within their stated time, or if no time is stated, within 30 days. If there is a delay, the seller must notify the buyer of the delay, and give the buyer an option to cancel the order for a full refund.

Of all the Federal Trade Commission laws, the Mail Order Merchandise Rule is the one the FTC is enforcing the most on Internet businesses. The FTC has received many complaints from customers, of delays in receiving merchandise, and of the frustration trying to reach Internet businesses to find out why merchandise hasn't been delivered, and when it will be delivered.

Your Web site will earn a lot of customer confidence and trust if you can tell your customers how long it takes to fill an order and how long it will take for delivery. Customers also like to know that the goods they ordered are in stock.

If you do include shipping information on your Web site, be careful with your wording. Your statement, once posted, becomes a legal contract your customers can hold you to. If you say, "We ship same day" or "We ship within 24 hours," you will be expected to live up to that claim. A statement such as, "We usually ship within 24 hours," gives you an out, and still sounds like good service.

**Labeling.** Packages and labels must conform to the Federal Fair Packaging and Labeling Act. Basically, a label must identify the product, list the manufacturer, packer, or distributor, and show the net quantity, both inch/pound and metric. The Act specifies how the label must be printed and where on the goods it must appear.

**Advertising.** Advertising may not be deceptive or misleading. You must have a reasonable basis for all advertising claims. You must have evidence to support your claims. Environmental benefits cannot be exaggerated. If you say its free, it must be free.

Be very careful in wording your advertising. Don't make any claims you cannot support. If your Web site claims that "studies show..." or "experts prefer..." something or other, you are required by law to have copies of the studies and documented statements from the experts. Be especially careful about medical and health claims, as the government tends to crack down on these advertisements the hardest.

Of particular concern to the Federal Trade Commission is how and where advertising "fine print" (i.e. disclaimers) should appear on a Web site. The FTC is not pleased with sites that bury disclaimers on separate Web pages or that require buyers to scroll way down a page to find the information.

So far, the FTC's recommendations about disclaimers on Web sites are suggestions without the force of law. But other FTC laws have gone as far as legally requiring a certain size typeface, specific wording, and a specific location on a product or warranty card. It is likely we will soon see some 614-page FTC document full of legal requirements how to tell your customer that all sales are final.

The Federal Trade Commission has published a booklet, "Dot Com Disclosures," outlining their requirements and suggestions for online merchants. Available from their web site **www.ftc.gov**.

---

# Chapter 31:
# Employees and the Internet

*"This business of peeking over employees' shoulders is a lot more complicated. Just what kind of workplace do you want to create?"*
**—Kimberly Weisul, Business Week Magazine**

Employees are causing their employers no end of trouble over Internet access and use.

If you've ever taken a break, while doing work on the Internet, to check your personal e-mail, or visit some fun Web site, you can easily imagine how your employees might also be tempted to take a quick break from work and do their own Internet surfing. Employees who would never think of leaving work to run to the corner store or to the Post Office, think nothing of doing personal Internet business on company time. It's so easy and quick. It costs you money, and it could bring you all manner of problems.

If employees have access to the Internet at work, you should have a written policy, clearly known to every employee, regarding Internet use.

It is up to you how much or how little personal Internet use you'll allow. Will you allow Internet use during working hours, or only on breaks and lunch? Will you restrict the kind of use allowed? What if an employee is sitting at his desk during lunch, viewing a site that may be offensive to other employees or customers or visitors? What if someone accidently sees the site and is upset or embarrassed? What if an employee e-mails an off-color joke or a tasteless comment to another employee, who takes offense?

This may sound unlikely to you, but it has happened in many businesses, large and small. Businesses are often held liable for the actions of employees who send or view pornographic, defamatory, racist, sexually suggestive, or threatening materials. It has resulted in lawsuits, sexual harassment charges, bad publicity for the business, and bad morale among employees.

Hopefully you are on close enough terms with your employees to keep Internet vigils unnecessary. Most businesses, unfortunately, do not trust their employees, and feel the need to set up employee surveillance systems. The American Management Association reports that over three-quarters of U.S. companies say they actively monitor their worker's communications and on-the-job activities. It has not brought harmony to the workplace.

Most workers resent the fact that their employers are snooping. They view it as an invasion of their privacy. And it is, but the courts have ruled many times that employees do not have privacy rights on the job. If an employer feels that it is necessary to check up on employees, the employer has a legal right to monitor employee use of the computers. The employer has a legal right to read employees' e-mail.

This is definitely unfriendly territory. How is monitoring going to affect an employee's enthusiasm for coming to work? Sometimes just putting a no-privacy policy in writing as part of employee guidelines—without actually setting up or implementing any systems—will inspire employees not to misuse your computers. letting employees know they might be watched is often as effective as actually watching them. The "no film in the surveillance camera" approach.

If you feel the need to actually track employee use of computers and the Internet, there is software available that will let you set up monitoring systems. A less intrusive solution is filtering software, which blocks access to forbidden sites on the Internet. Filtering software, however, is far less than perfect.

It is your decision. If you do have an Internet policy, to avoid legal problems with your employees, be sure the policy is in writing, and get a signed statement from each employee that he or she has received a copy of the policy and has read it. A written policy not only establishes rules for your employees, it will help you should you ever find yourself in court due to an employee's misconduct. If an employer does not have a written policy, the courts are more likely to hold the employer to blame.

A written policy on personal Internet use should be carefully and specifically worded. If you use vague words such as "inappropriate" or "reasonable," you might as well have no written policy at all.

Explain to your employees that a written policy does not cast disparagement on them. The employees would not be there in the first place if the employer did not trust them. The policy protects the employer from "the next guy," the one you hire by mistake, and by the time you fire him three days later, the damage is done.

Even when employees are accessing the Internet with your permission, employees can unknowingly allow a virus or even a hacker into your computer system by doing something as harmless as checking their personal e-mail.

Employees should be instructed to never open an e-mail attachment unless they know ahead of time that an attachment is being sent from a legitimate source. (See **Chapter 20: Security**, for more about e-mail). Employees should not download files from chat-rooms or software from an unreliable source. Downloaded files and software can carry hidden viruses, infecting your computer as soon as the files are downloaded.

If employees understand the security risks associated with Internet use, they may be more cooperative and understanding of your policies.

## Security Measures for Employees

Give employees access only to the information they need to do their jobs. Every employee should have a password. Establish passwords that let people only into the areas you want them to be able to access. Keep passwords private, and change the passwords every 60 or 90 days.

Instruct employees to log off of networks, programs, and the Internet whenever they take a break or finish their work for the day.

Warn employees not to give out any passwords or confidential information over the telephone, or in person, to anybody the employee does not know. Hackers and information thieves often pose as corporate or government officials, representatives of Internet services or telephone companies, and even new hires, to get employees to give out private business information.

## When An Employee Leaves Your Employ

Many hackers and others causing problems with business computers are former employees with a grudge against the employer. Whenever an employee leaves your business, take precautions to be sure the former employee no longer has access to your company computer. Disable the employee's password. If the employee knew other employees' passwords, assign new passwords to the remaining employees.

**"It's shortsighted to skip legal measures you know you should take. You risk creating all kinds of potential problems for yourself down the road, especially if your company has real growth potential."**

*—Robert Tarutis, President, Tarutis Communications, Waltham, Ma.*

# Section Six:
# Intellectual Property

"Men seem more than ever prone to confuse
information with knowledge, and knowledge
with wisdom, and try to solve problems of life
in terms of engineering."

—T.S. Eliot

# Chapter 32:
# Intellectual Property

*"Once a party decides to make information available online, does that mean the party has an absolute right to expect the legal system to enforce any and all ownership claims the party chooses, to assert against all users?"*
**—George B. Delta, attorney, author, "Law of the Internet"**

Intellectual property, also known as intangible property, refers to copyrights, trademarks and patents. U.S. law has always recognized the commercial value of ideas, words and inventions. Laws protecting the rights of the creators of intellectual property have existed almost since the Declaration of Independence. In today's "knowledge economy" intellectual property is more valuable than ever. The patents that some Internet businesses own are more valuable than the businesses themselves.

Before the Internet, most small businesses did not pay much attention to intellectual property laws, and few businesses felt a need to protect their intellectual property rights. Businesses were mostly local, with little or no exposure to the world at large. Only publishers and artists were really concerned about copyright protection. Inventors sometimes filed for patents. Trademark law was something associated with famous brands.

But now, every business with a presence on the Internet is part of a global network, every business has global exposure, and every business must protect itself from intellectual property theft. Businesses on the Internet must also avoid unintentionally violating the intellectual property rights of others.

Regardless of the business you are in, if you are on the Internet, you should learn the basics of copyright, trademark, and patent law. But don't panic. The basics are not difficult to learn, they are covered right here.

# Chapter 33:
# Copyright

*"The Internet is one giant copying machine."*

**—PC Magazine**

United States copyright laws are the same on the Internet as every-where else. Almost everything on your Web site is protected by United States copyright law.

## What Can Be Copyrighted?

Just about everything that is your original creation can be copyrighted: Literary, dramatic, musical and artistic works. Writing, with specific exceptions listed below. Designs: clothing, architecture, jewelry, furniture, crafts. Business logos. Illustrations. Paintings. Slides. Photographs. Movies. Videos. Games. Puzzles. Models. Audio recordings. Maps. Ads. Brochures. Catalogs. Promotional materials.

Software can be copyrighted, both the code and the visible results. Some software can also be patented. See **Chapter 35: Patents**.

On your Web site, your product descriptions, company descriptions and business logo are protected by copyright law. Your entire Web site can be copyrighted, just as an entire book is copyrighted. Or one illustration on your Web site can be copyrighted, just as a painting can be copyrighted.

The content of a Web site is not the only aspect of the site protected by copyright. The overall design of a Web site, the "look" or appearance of the site, if it is original and unique, is often considered by the courts to be protected by copyright. If a Web site uses an original design theme—size, shape, color—for its click-on buttons, or for its navigation bar, or for other site functions, it is considered original artwork, protected by copyright.

In creating your Web site, you can borrow freely from other sites when designing overall layout and general appearance. These are "ideas" and are not copyrightable. Just don't use someone else's words or original artwork, or even something similar.

## What Cannot Be Copyrighted?

What cannot be copyrighted? Business and product names, domain names, and short slogans ("Fastest Paint Job in Porkchop Junction") cannot be copyrighted, although some names and phrases can be trademarked. (See **Chapter 34: Trademarks**.)

You cannot copyright contents or lists of ingredients. You can copyright a recipe if the recipe includes written original instructions, baking tips, etc., not just "heat oven to 350, grease pan," and the like.

You cannot copyright: Blank forms. Math tables. Rulers. Standard calendars. Height or weight charts. Titles. Short phrases. Slogans. Familiar symbols or sayings.

Ideas and concepts cannot be copyrighted. You can write about ideas and concepts and copyright the writing. A description of a machine could be copyrighted as a writing, but this will not prevent others from making or using the machine.

You cannot copyright someone else's work, new or old, unless the copyright holder, estate or heirs, gives permission. You can reproduce old works that are no longer protected by copyright (works in the "public domain") but you cannot claim a copyright for them unless you have made significant alterations, in effect creating new original work based on the older work.

## Basic Copyright Rights

The owner of a copyright has exclusive rights to print and copy the work including the right to download it and put it on a Web site; to sell or distribute copies of the work, including the right to e-mail it or broadcast it on the Internet; to dramatize, record or translate the work; to perform or broadcast the work publicly.

Under copyright law, a copyright automatically belongs to the creator of a work, with a few important exceptions. Under what's called the "work for hire" law, if the creator of a work is an employee (an individual on your payroll, not someone who is self-employed), the copyright and all rights to the work belong to the employer, none to the employee.

If a work is specially ordered or commissioned, rights to the work may belong to the creator or may belong to the person hiring the creator, depending on the nature of the work. Details about commissioned work are on the Copyright Office Web page **www.lcweb.loc.gov/copyright**. To be entirely clear and legal about copyright ownership, the creator and the commissioner of a work should stipulate in a written contract who owns the copyright.

This is especially important for Web site owners who contract with independent Web designers. A work created by an independent designer or outside company might legally belong to the designer, and not to the Web site owner who paid for the work. Web site owners should make it very clear, in a written contract, that the site owner, not the designer, has full ownership of the work and retains all rights to the work. This is covered in **Chapter 19: Web Designer Contract**.

## Copyrighted Databases

At present, compiled listings of information such as addresses and telephone numbers, stock quotes, business trade directories, lists of magazines by subject, etc., are not protected by copyright. But as more Web sites offer these listings, Congress is considering new copyright laws to prohibit the exact duplication of such databases. Such new copyright laws, if passed, and if they stand up in the courts when challenged, would prohibit exact reproduction of a database but would allow enhancement, rearrangement and reuse of the information.

## Altered Material

It is easy to copy an illustration, photograph, or design off a Web site, and using design software, alter the original material to an extent that it isn't recognizable. Most (but not all) copyright experts feel this is in violation of copyright laws. The creator of the work owns the copyright not just on the original work but also to any altered version of the work. But the courts don't always agree. And even when the courts do agree, it is very difficult to discover such an altered work, and it is difficult to prove it was originally your work.

So what do you do? You tell people that the work is yours, it is copyrighted by you, and it may not be reproduced or altered without your permission. And hope people will be honest and respect your rights. Most of them will.

## Acquiring a Copyright

Within the United States, copyright protection automatically exists from the moment a work is created. You are not required to put a copyright notice on the work, although the U.S. Copyright Office strongly recommends that you do. A copyright notice will eliminate the possibility that someone will innocently help themselves to your work, thinking it isn't protected.

The copyright notice should include the word "copyright" or the symbol ©, the year, and your name or your business name. You can use a pseudonym, assumed name, or pen name if you prefer. For copyright protection, a fictitious name is just as legal as your real name. You can leave the year off the copyright notice if you don't want people to know the year of copyright, although this will weaken copyright protection in some foreign countries. Some foreign countries also require the words "All rights reserved" on your copyright notice. (Foreign copyright protection—or lack of it—is covered below.) Repeat the basic copyright notice on every page of your Web site: copyright, year, name.

To receive maximum legal protection in the United States, your copyright must be registered with the U.S. Copyright Office. You fill out a simple form, pay a $30 fee, and send the U.S. Copyright Office two printed-out copies of whatever it is you are copyrighting. You can copyright the entire contents of your Web site, using one copyright form, paying one fee. It's that easy. The Copyright Office will accept printed-on-paper copies or CD-ROMs, but they will not accept floppy disks.

You can file for a copyright at any time. The sooner you file, the sooner you have the added legal protection. Filing the legal papers with the U.S. Copyright Office is your best proof that you own a copyright should someone steal your work and claim it as their own. But again, remember that you legally own your copyright whether you file the forms with the U.S. Copyright Office or not.

If you make significant revisions or updates to your copyrighted material, you should fill out new copyright forms and re-register your copyright with the Copyright Office. Each revision is another $30, so you don't want to re-register your work just for minor changes. Your original copyright is still valid.

A copyright is good for your lifetime plus seventy years. It is not renewable, unless it is a revision or update.

For information and forms: Register of Copyrights, Library of Congress, Washington, DC 20559. **www.lcweb.loc.gov/copyright**. You can download the forms and instructions, but you must mail in your completed form and payment. The Copyright Office does not accept filled-in forms or payment over the Internet.

## Protecting Your Web Site Copyright

Under United States copyright law, no one else may copy, reproduce, distribute, sell, broadcast, or even e-mail any part of your Web site without your permission. But people do it all the time. Material is too easy to steal off the Internet.

Many people who "borrow" material from a web site do not fully realize that they are stealing. People think of the Internet as a place where everything is free, including your hard work. Quite often, just reminding your visitors that everything on your web site is copyrighted, and that copying is not permitted, will stop many of them from taking anything.

However, many businesses *want* people to download and print their Web sites. The sites double as catalogs. People who download the Web pages will have the pages to refer to after they log off the Internet—and can't find you again because they forgot your domain name. These businesses often put a copyright notice on the Web site but do not warn visitors not to copy the Web pages.

If you find that someone has taken anything from your Web site and put it on their own Web site, you can send a "cease and desist" letter, notifying the infringer that such use is illegal, demand that the material be removed from the infringer's Web site, and suggest that failure to comply can result in legal action. Quite often such a letter is all you need to end the problem.

The tone of the letter can have quite an effect on the infringer's response. Being polite but firm is often more successful than being belligerent, rude or accusatory. A cease-and-desist letter does not commit you in any way to legal action, it can be a bluff. But be sure to keep a copy of the letter and any response, should you decide in the future to talk to a lawyer.

## Technological Copyright Protection

Posting a copyright notice and reminding people not to copy your work will stop many people from downloading, printing and reproducing any-thing that catches their eye. But there are people who don't care and who will help themselves to whatever they want from the Internet.

There is software known as "digital rights management" (DRM) software, that will help protect the contents of your Web site from un-authorized copying and downloading. Password access, encryption, digital watermarks, and lock-down technology are different terms for different ways to limit access and use of your site and its contents.

Watermarks put an imprint into a sound or image file that doesn't let unauthorized users reproduce clean copies. A watermarked image may have the domain name or copyright owner displayed across the page when printed, saved to a hard drive, or transferred to another site. Much like branding cattle, watermarking is a deterrent to theft as well as a good tool to track down pirates. Watermarking may lead Web surfers back to your site if they find your images on another site.

Another technology, called a "digital object identifier" (DOI), works much like a watermark. It attaches a coded label to whatever you are trying to protect. The DOI label stays with the content no matter where it gets hijacked to.

Encryption software scrambles data and gives access only to people who have a password or pay a fee to unscramble the data.

Depending on your needs and budget, you can acquire software that will deny people access to the Web site or part of the Web site. You can allow Web surfers to view your site without the ability to copy, print, capture or save the content. Software is available that allows people to browse preview content and pay for additional content.

You can also get software that searches the Internet for Web sites that have taken content off your Web site and placed it on their sites.

Companies that offer Web site protection software advertise regularly in business, computer and Internet magazines, and can be found on the Internet using search engines.

No technology will stop a determined hacker, but few Web sites have to deal with such mad scientists. Just as most thieves can be deterred simply by locking a door, most Web pirates can be thwarted with simple protection methods. There's plenty easy pickings on the Web, no need for some reprobate to spend a lot of time trying to decode your site.

## Selling and Licensing Your Copyrighted Material

When someone buys something from you that you created and for which you own the copyright, such as a book, a photograph, music, software, the purchaser does not acquire the right to reproduce the work. The purchaser has the right to resell that single copy, just as someone can sell a used book or CD, but not to sell multiple copies. Nor can the purchaser use your work in another work to be offered for sale.

Control and protection of a copyrighted work is difficult. This problem has grown with the Internet and the ease of duplicating and broadcasting someone else's work.

Many copyright owners try to strengthen their legal rights, and impress their rights upon the people who acquire their work, by "licensing" their works rather than selling them. The purchaser does not actually buy the work, he buys the right to keep and use the work, according to a licensing agreement. In this way, the owner of the work defines the limits of the usage of the work, and can demand broader protections for the work than basic copyright protection.

Almost all software manufacturers "license" their software to users.

You did not buy that software you thought you bought. You bought the right to use the software, according to the terms of the licensing agreement that came with it. This is the manufacturer's way of legally maintaining control of software misuse, such as unauthorized duplication.

Take a look at one of the licensing agreements that came with any software you purchased or downloaded, to get an idea how the software manufacturer wants to control the use and reproduction of its software. These licensing agreements, like the "terms and conditions" agreements demanded by many Web services, are standard fill-in-the-blank agreements, everybody using almost the exact same words.

Software manufacturers, not satisfied with licensing agreements, have gone even further to protect their rights. They have urged several states to pass a law called the Uniform Computer Information Transactions Act, UCITA for short. This onerous piece of legislation basically allows the software manufacturers to revoke your "license" to use their software if you violate the licensing agreement. If you violate the agreement, the manufacturers, under the UCITA law, can actually reach right into your hard drive and disable the software.

Most likely you will never encounter UCITA or a software manufacturer breaking and entering your computer. If a piece of software vanishes from your computer, chances are it's just your computer being a computer (or your kid pushed the wrong buttons).

Just as you acquire licensing rights to software you acquire, you can sell licensing rights to your own products or to content on your Web site, instead of selling the products outright.

If you are offering a license instead of a sale, the information should be displayed prominently on your Web site. A license should spell out, in detail, the scope of the rights being granted: what can be done with the licensed material, how it can or cannot be copied or shared, if it can be altered, whether it can be resold or not, and if it is for a specified time period. The license should follow, as closely as possibly, industry norms. Read the licenses offered on other Web sites and use them as a guide to writing yours.

## The Digital Millennium Copyright Act

There is one U.S. copyright law that applies specifically to the Internet and computer software. The Digital Millennium Copyright Act includes these provisions:

1. Internet Service Providers (ISPs) are not liable for copyright infringement committed by the ISP's customers (Web sites hosted by the ISP, and individuals and businesses that use the ISP to access the Net) if the ISP is not aware of the infringement or lacks the ability to control the illegal activities.

2. Copyrighted computer programs can be duplicated for purposes of maintenance and repair.

3. Some Web sites have programming built into their copyrighted material that prevents unauthorized access and unauthorized copying of the material. The Digital Millennium Copyright Act prohibits the creation, use, or sale of a device or computer program that circumvents the programming used by copyright owners to protect their material. There are some exceptions to this law to allow for what's commonly known as "fair use" (limited free use) of copyrighted material.

4. Web broadcasters, in certain circumstances, can digitally record copyrighted material for use in a broadcast.

## International Copyright Protection

The World Wide Web is just that, world wide, and your Web site is accessible to Web surfers—and to thieves—from anywhere in the world.

There is no such thing as an international copyright that will protect you throughout the entire world. Protection against unauthorized use in a particular country depends on the national laws of that country. Over 100 countries have signed treaties with the United States honoring U.S. copyright law. But many countries did not sign any treaty, and in fact some countries offer absolutely no copyright protection to any foreign works.

copyright law. But many countries did not sign any treaty, and in fact some countries offer absolutely no copyright protection to any foreign works.

If you are concerned about copyright protection in a specific country, you should find out the degree of protection, if any, available to U.S. copyright holders. If possible, this should be done before your Web site is up and running, because protection may depend on the facts existing at the time the Web site first came online.

The U.S. Copyright Office publishes a free guide, Circular 38-A, "International Copyright Relations of the United States," which includes a list of countries that maintain copyright relationships with the United States. Circular 38-A is available through the mail (Register of Copyrights, Library of Congress, Washington, DC 20559) or from the U.S. Copyright Office Web site **www.lcweb.loc.gov/copyright**.

## Infringing on Someone Else's Copyright

If you take anything off of someone else's Web site and put it on your own Web site, without first getting written permission, you are violating their copyright. Quite often, however, a Web site owner will be very happy to let you reproduce the contents of the site, if it will benefit that site. It never hurts to ask. When you get an okay, be sure to keep a written copy of the approval, for your own protection.

There are murkier areas of copyright infringement you should be aware of. One possible problem concerns links. The problem can occur if your site provides a link to another site: a visitor to your Web site your clicks on the link, and the visitor is immediately transferred to the linked site. This may seem totally harmless, but some sites may not want links to their Web sites. Sites that are linked without their approval have been known to claim copyright infringement. This is covered in **Chapter 18: Web Site Design**.

# Chapter 34:
# Trademarks

*"It's much harder to create a brand on the Web than anywhere else. People thought it would be easier because it's free, but that makes it harder because everybody is doing it."*
                    **—Larry Kramer, CEO, CBS MarketWatch**

A trademark gives you the right, with some limitations, to exclusive use of your business name, product name, brand name or other identifying words or symbols.

A trademark is a word, name, brand, slogan or expression, a symbol, shape, design or logo, a color or combination of colors, a unique sound, or some combination of these, adopted by a business to identify its goods and distinguish them from goods manufactured or sold by others.

You cannot usually get a trademark for your own name, or for a geographical name, such as "Southwest." You cannot trademark expressions already in common use, such as "Have a Nice Day." You cannot have a trademark that is so similar to another trademark it could confuse people.

You cannot trademark words that actually describe your product. A window manufacturer cannot trademark the name "Windows" for its windows, but obviously, a software company can trademark a product called "Windows."

Trademarks are not functional. They serve no useful purpose other than to identify goods or services. Trademarks do not protect the actual products. A trademark will protect your brand name but not the product bearing your brand name. Copyrights and patents serve that purpose.

No two companies selling the same or similar products or services can use the same trademark. Two or more different companies can use the same trademark, if their products or services are completely unrelated, and if people will not be confused as to whose trademark is whose. Apple Record Company and Apple Computer Company, for example, peacefully co-exist, both with valid trademarks for the name Apple.

However, large corporations that own famous name trademarks, McDonalds for example, often are able to stop all other businesses from using the same or similar trademarks. Even if the other "McDonalds" or "MacDonalds" or even "Big Mac's" couldn't possibly be mistaken for the McDonalds fast food chain, McDonalds can invoke what's called "famous trademark protection" (also known as "trademark dilution") to force other companies from using anything remotely resembling McDonalds.

## Trademarks and Domain Names

Domain names can be trademarked, but the same trademark rules apply. To be able to trademark your domain name, the domain name must be more than just the name of your business or an online address. It must be a brand of sorts, used in commerce as a commercial identifier. It must be promoted to the public and used by consumers.

Generic domain names, like generic product names, cannot be trademarked. An Internet toy business can have a domain name called toys.com, but the business could not trademark the name, because it is generic, it describes the product. You can get a trademark for original and multi-word domain names, such as razzledazzletoys.com. You can get a trademark for distinctive domain names without any obvious meaning, the very successful tactic used by Amazon.com and Yahoo.

In trademark law, multiple owners of the same trademark can co-exist as long as they are not providing the same goods and services. But the domain name system permits only one registrant to use a particular domain name. On the Internet, trademark law has caused a great deal of trouble over domain names.

Conflicts often occur when someone owns a domain name on the Internet and someone else owns a trademark to that same name. Large corporations, who once didn't care if some small business in Tumbleweed, Oklahoma, had the same business name, don't want these small businesses showing up on Internet search engines when someone types in "Subway" or "Ford" or whatever the corporation's name or product is.

Federal law prohibits people from registering a domain name that is someone else's registered trademark. If your domain name is even similar to a trademarked name, similar enough to possibly cause confusion, the trademark owner may be able to force you to give up the domain name.

If a trademark is not officially registered, or if a trademark was registered after the domain name was claimed by someone else, or if two businesses own the same trademark name, or if one of the claimants is outside the United States, Internet policy, which is not governed by U.S. laws, gets unpredictable. A business may or may not be able to force someone else to abandon their domain name.

If the owner of a trademark acquired trademark rights before you acquired your domain name, the courts usually rule in favor of the trademark owner. If the trademark was acquired after you acquired your domain name, you have a legal argument in your favor—assuming you want to spend the time and money to make your argument.

Regardless of "who came first," if a trademark owner notifies Internic, the organization that assigns rights to domain names, or notifies one of the businesses licensed to register domain names, such as Network Solutions, that your domain name infringes on their trademark, the domain name registrar can take the domain name away from you and put it on hold, preventing anyone from using it, until legal ownership is determined.

Many trademark owners, aware of this problem, have acquired ownership of all domain names that are the same as, or very similar to, their trademark names. So it is more and more unlikely that you will accidently find yourself in the unenviable position of having someone's trademark as your domain name. But you should research your domain name carefully, to try to prevent a trademark dispute.

Internet trademark disputes have arisen when a Web site uses someone else's trademark in its meta-tags. Meta-tags are hidden words inserted in a Web site's programming, words that are not visible on the Web site and not seen by Web users. (You can see a Web site's meta-tags by clicking "view page source" on the browser). Search engines read the meta-tags as part of the process of evaluating and listing Web sites. Trademark owners have successfully stopped Web sites from putting trademarks in the meta-tags.

## Acquiring a Trademark

The first step to acquiring a trademark is to find out if anyone else already owns the trademark. The U.S. Patent and Trademark Office has a free online listing of registered trademarks, the Trademark Electronic Search System (TESS): **www.tess.uspto.gov**. You should also check trade directories, product catalogs and other business listings, looking for unregistered, but still valid trademarks.

You acquire a basic trademark right, with limited legal protection, simply by creating and using your trademark. You acquire stronger and more easily defended legal rights to a trademark by registering with the U.S. Patent & Trademark Office.

Federal trademark registration gives you protection throughout the United States, but it is only available to trademarks that are used in interstate or international commerce. You must be doing business across state lines or your product must cross state lines in the normal course of business. This certainly will apply to all Web sites. Federal trademark rights are not international.

## Registering a Federal Trademark

If you have thought up a trademark you want to use but are not yet using the trademark, you can file an Intent To Use application for your trademark. This protects your trademark until you actually use it. The Intent To Use application is good for six months, and can be renewed every six months for up to three years. The application and each renewal costs $100. An Intent To Use Application is effective immediately upon paying the fee.

Once you are actually using a trademark, you can apply for regular trademark registration. The fee is $245. This fee is in addition to any fees you paid with the Intent To Use application.

You can file Intent to Use applications and regular trademark applications online, using the Trademark Office's Trademark Electronic Application System (TEAS) at **www.uspto.gov**. You pay the fees online with the application, using a credit card.

You do not immediately get a registered trademark when you file your application. Your application is examined by the Trademark Office, to make sure it meets trademark requirements and to make sure no one else has registered the trademark. You can track your application as it moves through the approval process, on the Trademark Office Web site.

Initial trademark registration remains in force for ten years, but you must file something called a Declaration of Use Statement between the fifth and sixth years. The trademark may then be renewed every ten years, for as long as you like.

The familiar ® symbol means that a trademark or service mark is officially registered with the U.S. Trademark Office, and full legal protection has been secured. The equally familiar ™ symbol is a formal notice that you are claiming ownership of a trademark but have not registered it. The ™ symbol can be used even if no federal trademark application is pending. Using this symbol, however, does not provide the full legal protection accorded a registered ® trademark.

For more information: **www.uspto.gov**.

## Protecting Your Trademark

In order to keep your trademark, you must actively promote and protect it. You must identify your trademark, with the ® symbol if the trademark is officially registered with the Patent and Trademark Office, or with the ™ symbol if the trademark is not registered. You must mention on your Web page, and in your catalogs and advertisements that your trademark is in fact a trademark, and you own the rights to it.

You must use "due diligence" to monitor your trademark. That is, you must do a reasonable amount of snooping to make sure no one else is using your trademark. On the Internet, you must occasionally check for other Web sites that use your trademark, most likely innocently, not even knowing you own the trademark rights. You must notify the infringing Web site immediately that you are legal owner of the trademark, and request that the site stop using it. If you do not put in a prompt complaint, you could lose your right to stop the other site's use of the trademark.

If you do not use your trademark for two or more years, it is considered abandoned. Anyone else can claim and use the trademark. Use it or lose it.

## Additional Protection For Your Domain Name

Whether you have a trademark or not, the best way to protect your company name is to make it well known and easy to find. Get listed in every business, trade, association, and phone directory that offer free listings (plenty do; don't pay for a listing). Get publicity. Make it as hard as possible for new businesses not to have heard of you. People don't maliciously steal business names, they just don't know you're there.

Even if you don't have a trademark, you have legal recourse against people who are intentionally using confusingly similar domain names.

The federal Lanham Act, also known as the False Advertising Statute, prohibits people from using domain names that cause confusion, mistakes, or deception as to the origin of the Web site. This Act is aimed at people who willfully and in bad faith, set up a domain name deceptively similar to another site. The Act does not protect generic domain names. For example, if you sell guitars and your Web site is www.guitars.com, someone else who sells guitars could have a Web site named www.guitar.com.

## Using Someone Else's Trademark

If you are selling someone else's product, you probably will have no problems if you use their trademark—name, logo, slogan—as part of the description of the product. But you may be prohibited from using the product's trademark name as part of your domain name, or in your hidden meta tags. Some corporations do not want Web sites using their name, even sites selling their products. The corporations want all Web surfers to find their own Web site, not some retailer's site.

This has become a serious problem for some businesses that sell a certain brand or product exclusively, such as new car dealerships, especially businesses whose name includes the brand name of the goods you are selling (for example, a store that sells nothing but Levi's jeans called The Levi's Connection). This has also become a problem for some franchise businesses, where the franchisor has prohibited franchisees from using certain domain names, wanting to reserve them for its own Web sites. See **Chapter 12: Franchise Businesses**.

If you want to include a trademarked famous brand name as part of your domain name, I suggest you get written permission from the trademark holder. Many corporations will probably be happy to see their name all over the Internet, while others won't.

If you are only describing trademarked products that you're selling, but not as a part of your domain name, you can take the cautious route and get permission, or you probably can just go ahead and mention the products and figure you'll not have a problem.

One serious word of caution: If you are speaking unkindly of someone's trademarked product, or if you are comparing the product as inferior to another product, look out. These trademark owners check the Internet regularly for mentions of their products. If they find a disparaging comment, you will hear from their lawyers. The Federal Trade Commission says that any claims you make about a product, pro or con, must be supported by documented proof. This is not any fun. You have little to gain and a lot to lose by speaking negatively about someone else's product.

## International Trademarks

Federal trademark rights are not international. The same trademark can be owned by other companies in other countries. U.S. trademark law applies only in the United States. Other countries have their own laws. The issue of domain name ownership versus foreign trademarks is an untested area. If your domain name turns out to be a trademarked name owned by a foreign corporation, you may well find yourself in your very own international crisis.

# Chapter 35:
# Patents

*"Everything that can be invented has been invented."*
**—Charles Duell, U.S. Commissioner of Patents, 1901**

The Internet has dramatically changed the world of patents and patent law. People are inventing on their computers instead of in their garage, and the U.S. Patent Office is struggling to keep up with new technologies.

The biggest, and most contentious, patent issues involve business software and business methods used on the Internet. For the first time in the history of the U.S. Patent Office, patents are being issued to companies that devise new, and mostly computer-programmed, ways of doing business.

Companies that have created software to navigate Web sites, acquire customers, process orders, offer different pricing methods, and other variations of doing business on the Internet, are being issued patents for these processes. Very often, the companies are simply translating basic business practices into computer code, and getting patents on their systems. The companies obtaining the patents are aggressively trying to stop other businesses from using similar business methods on the Internet, or demanding licensing fees from the other companies.

If you set up a Web site that uses a system for processing orders similar to one set up and patented by, say, Amazon.com, you may one day hear from Amazon's lawyers, if they happen to find you, and if they feel you are worth their time and trouble.

My guess is that, unless you grow very large, you will never hear from anyone accusing you of using their patented system. I personally would set up my Web page however I like, and not worry about it.

The courts and Congress may soon rescue you, and every other Web entrepreneur using basic business methods that someone programmed for the Internet and grabbed a patent. The courts are currently ruling on lawsuits aimed at nullifying some of the broader business-method patents. The Business Method Patent Improvement Act, if it becomes law, will severely limit overly broad patents and patents for traditional business methods that are merely converted to digital codes.

## Getting Your Own Patent

Internet business-method patents—and all other kinds of patents—are being filed every day. If you have a new Internet idea, or a new real-world invention, you should consider the pros and cons of patents.

There are three types of patents: utility patents, design patents, and plant patents. The type of patent described here is the utility patent, a patent for an "invention." An invention is a machine; or something that can be manufactured; or a process, which is what Internet business patents are. A patent can be issued for a new invention or for a new and useful improvement of an older patented invention.

To qualify for a patent, your "invention" must meet these requirements:

1. The invention must be "novel," which means that the invention is new, materially different from any previous patents issued by the U.S. Patent and Trademark Office (the PTO).

2. The invention must be "useful," which the PTO defines as "a significant use must exist."

3. The invention must be "non-obvious" to a person with "ordinary skill" in your field.

4. The invention must work. It must function for its intended purpose.

5. A patent will not be granted if the invention was in public use or on sale more than a year before filing the patent application, or if the invention was described in a publication more than a year before filing the application.

6. An idea alone cannot be patented. You must have a detailed written description or drawings of your invention.

7. Software that simply solves mathematical problems is not eligible for a patent. The software must "do" something, make something happen, not just compute numbers.

## Patent Rights

Unlike copyrights and trademarks, patent rights are not automatically granted just because you created an invention. You must apply to the U.S. Patent and Trademark Office to apply for a patent. Full patent rights come into existence only on approval of your application.

A patent gives an inventor the right to prevent others from manufacturing, using or selling the invention in the United States, for twenty years. The twenty year time period starts on the date the patent application was filed. The twenty years includes the time it takes for the patent to be approved, which itself can take anywhere from several months to several years. So the actual time your patent is valid may be a lot less than 20 years. After a patent is issued, you must pay periodic government maintenance fees throughout the life of the patent. Once a patent's 20-year life has expired, the patent may not be renewed or extended. Anyone can use an invention after the patent expires.

It is important to understand what legal rights a patent offers. The law says that a patent give you the exclusive right "to prevent" others from using your patent. This means that it is up to you to find the culprit, and the burden of proof is on you to prove that the thief really did steal your idea. This is not easy and it is not cheap. But a patent will keep an honest inventor from getting a patent on the same or similar invention. Stopping a thief may be near impossible, but stopping another inventor should be easy. This is the greatest value in a patent: letting other inventors know that their new invention has already been created by someone else.

A patent can be sold to a large company, a company with the financial resources to produce and sell the invention, and with the legal muscle to stop thieves. For an inventor interested in selling or licensing his invention to a large company, if the inventor patents the invention before offering it for sale, the invention is more marketable and less likely to be stolen by the larger company itself. I think it was the Prophet Jeremiah—or maybe Richard Nixon—who said, "No honor among thieves."

## Before Applying For A Patent

As you design and perfect your invention, keep a detailed record of the steps, a technical diary of sorts, with dates. Before building and testing the invention, make a full and clear written description, sign and date it, and have it notarized. This gives you some legal rights and protection under the "First To Invent" clause in U.S. patent law. No patent application need be filed to get the First To Invent protection.

As an alternative, you can pay a small fee and file an Invention Disclosure Document with the U.S. Patent Office, which the Office will keep on file for two years. This Document is not a patent application, merely an official record that you are working on an invention. This can be very helpful if you are in a dispute with another inventor (or company) over who was the first person to think up this new idea.

## Applying For a Patent

Applying for a patent can be a lengthy and expensive procedure. The government charges filing, issuance, and maintenance fees, and sometimes fees for printing and claims work. You may need help from a patent attorney or agent. And you have to "stand in line:" The U.S. Patent Office has over a half million active patent applications moving, glacially, through the system. But any dedicated inventor who is willing to study the laws, do the research, and struggle through the forms, will be able to patent his or her own invention at a fraction of the usual cost.

You can file patent applications online. The U.S. Patent Office's Electronic Patent Application Filing System (EFS) includes forms, instructions, and free software to help you prepare your application: **www.uspto.gov/ebc/index.html**. You can use the same Web site to track your application through the entire patent process.

Inventors who are unsure that their invention justifies the work and cost of going through the regular patent process have another option. They can file a Provisional Patent Application (a PPA), which is a temporary form of patent-pending. A PPA requires a lot less time, money and paperwork than a regular patent application, yet offers full patent-pending protection for one full year. By the end of the year's time, if things are looking promising, you can apply for a regular patent. But you have to start the patent application process all over again.

The Provisional Patent Application itself does not lead to a patent. Should you decide to proceed with the patent, you are spending more time and money, because you took the additional step of filling a Provisional Patent Application. But you do get an extra year's protection. You get the full twenty years, in addition to the PPA's year.

## Patent Pending / Patent Applied For

Products that have federal patent protection from the U.S. Patent & Trademark Office, are said to be "patented." A different term, "patent pending" (or "patent applied for") means that a patent application or a Provisional Patent Application has been filed but no patent has been issued yet. "Patent applied for" and "patent pending" are formal notices, but they offer little legal protection.

Some people use "patent pending" even though they haven't applied for anything, either to try to scare off imitators or to impress customers. This is illegal.

## Other Options

If filing for and obtaining a patent is a bit overwhelming or too expensive, there are other options. Many inventors simply produce and market their invention without a patent, run with it while it's hot, and not worry about someone stealing the idea. Particularly when you are dealing with rapidly changing technology, it's possible your product could become obsolete before anyone has time to copy it.

Many inventors sell or license their ideas to reputable manufacturing companies, companies that will patent the invention on behalf of, or in partnership with, the inventor. Should you approach such a company, have them sign a confidentiality nondisclosure statement before you show them your idea. Be sure to keep detailed, signed, and dated records of your invention as outlined above, which gives you protection under the First To Invent law.

Be wary of product development companies and invention marketing services, companies that charge you a fee to appraise your invention and make recommendations, but rarely offer any real help to get your patent issued or to earn you any money. I suggest that you stay away from such companies.

For more information about patents, write the U.S. Patent & Trademark Office, Washington, D.C. 20231. Telephone toll free 1-800-786-9199. On the Internet at **www.uspto.gov**.

**The first U.S. Patent, Patent #1, was issued in 1790 to Samuel Hopkins, for a process for making soap. Patent #1,000,000 was issued in 1911 to Francis H. Holton for a "vehicle tire." Patent #6,000,000 was issued on December 7, 1999, to 3Com Corporation, for "extendable method and apparatus for synchronizing multiple files on two different computer systems."**

# Section Seven:
# International Commerce

# Chapter 36:
# The "World Wide" Web

*"These days an office isn't so much a location as it is a state of mind."*
—**Karen Solomon, Business Start Ups Magazine**

The Internet has no geographical boundaries, which presents even the smallest Internet business the opportunity to find customers from all over the world, something impossible for many businesses before the creation of the Internet. It also presents the headaches of international laws and export restrictions, and the need for cultural education, previously of no concern to most businesses.

Most businesses in the United States are so U.S.-centered that we don't think of the Internet as a global marketplace. "www" really does stand for *World Wide* Web. If a company is on the Internet, it is global without necessarily planning to be. Sort of an "Extra Added Attraction," but only if you make it easy enough for overseas customers to contact you and purchase from you.

## Lost in the Translation

Few businesses will bother to translate their Web sites into foreign languages. But doing so can add immeasurably to your customer base, not just in foreign countries, but in the United States where many thousands of people are more comfortable—and more trusting—of a Web site when they can read it in Spanish or French or another language they grew up with.

Translating your site can bring all kinds of problems, if the translation is inaccurate, or if slang English words and expressions translate to something you didn't exactly mean.

This is especially a problem for domain names and brand names that are made up words. Many people have heard the famous story of Chevrolet's Nova car. When Chevrolet started advertising in Latin America, they discovered that "nova" means "no go" in Spanish. A large e-commerce site named Evite.com discovered too late that in French and Spanish "evite" is almost identical to a word that means "shun" or "avoid." If you choose a homemade name, you may first want to check other languages to make sure it doesn't mean "up yours" or "we're crooks" in German or Portuguese.

Many toll-free numbers do not work outside of the United States. If you list your toll-free number, include your regular phone number as well. When listing a phone number on your Web site, you may want to include the U.S. country code (which is 1). If your phone number spells out a cute expression (1-444-BUY-THIS), include the actual numbers, because overseas phones often lack letters on the keypad.

If you offer free or flat rate shipping to U.S. customers, you may want to have a different shipping charge for overseas. Many Web sites ask overseas customers to send an e-mail, and the site's owner quotes shipping for each order.

Don't force users to fill in a ZIP code or postal code; some countries don't have one. When typing in a date, use the names of the months instead of numbers. "4/6/01" means April 6 in the United states, but means June 4 in other countries.

---

# Chapter 37:
# U.S. Export Laws

*"What we're seeing, are overseas consumers ordering a book or CD over the Internet, and suddenly have to pay other charges they didn't know about. This is not a problem yet, but once global Internet trade takes off, we expect consumer purchases to be a big problem for us. Customs clearance is a major bottleneck to global trade."*
**—Harold Schoenfelder, European Managing Director, FedEx**

Most businesses can export goods without any formal permission. An export license is usually not required.

To ship a package out of the United States, you will need to fill out a customs form, which you can get at any post office, or from your UPS or FedEx delivery driver.

The Post Office has two customs forms, the shorter Form #2976 for packages that weigh under 4 pounds, and longer Form #2976-A for packages that weight 4 pounds or more. You pay nothing to fill out the forms, and there are no U.S. customs charges.

## Export Licenses

Some businesses must get an export license and a shipping document called a Shippers Export Declaration (SED) to ship goods to another country. Export licenses and SEDs are required for certain "strategic" goods, usually those with military uses, but also some high-tech hardware and software. Export licenses and SEDs are also required for goods shipped to certain "restricted" countries.

The U.S. Bureau of Export Administration (the BXA), which is part of the U.S. Department of Commerce, maintains a list of strategic goods and restricted countries. You can get full information on their Web site: **www.bxa.doc.gov**.

## Customs Duties

You, the shipper, do not pay any customs duties. But your overseas customers may have to pay customs or import duties when they receive the goods. The customer's own country, not the United States, decides what duties, if any, the customer must pay.

Your overseas customers may not be aware that they have to pay customs or import duties, which can sometimes as much as double the price of the goods. Although this can be a serious problem for international customers, I have never seen a single Web site that warns international customers about possible customs duties.

# Chapter 38:
# International Payment

*"Technology development is not as valuable as a nuts-and-bolts retail strategy."*
        —**Barry Parr, E-commerce Research Director, IDC Corp.**

One of the benefits of accepting credit cards is that you can take orders from overseas customers without concerning yourself with foreign currencies or currency conversions. You charge your overseas customer's credit card in U.S. dollars, and your credit card company pays you in U.S. dollars. The credit card company converts the U.S. dollars to the customer's currency and bills the customer in British pounds or Japanese yen or Canadian dollars or whatever currency the customer uses. You never see the conversion, and you do not pay any extra fees.

If you are making business-to-business sales to overseas customers, where you are not being paid with a credit card, much more complicated payment arrangements are required.

## Selling to Overseas Businesses

The Internet lets you promote your products not just to overseas customers, but also to overseas businesses that may be in a better position to sell your products to overseas customers.

Retail customers in France, for example, are much more likely to purchase from a French business than from one in the U.S. The French government is probably much more cooperative with an Internet site in France than one in the United States. A French Internet business will know local customs, local business practices, how local people like to shop, how to word a product description so it is appealing to local people.

Instead of trying to sell your products one at a time to overseas customers, you may want to explore the Internet to find overseas businesses that want to purchase your goods, or license the right to reproduce your goods, and sell the goods in their own country. This kind of international commerce, often referred to as a strategic partnership, is very common with both large and small businesses.

If you do find an overseas business to handle your products, it is extremely important that you learn about international laws, U.S. export requirements, and how to process a shipment to another country. While you may have no trouble sending one item overseas to a retail customer, you are guaranteed to have a lot of trouble sending a large shipment if it does not meet, exactly, all the requirements of all the governments, shippers, banks, and everyone else involved in the transaction. You need to learn about standard payment terms, letters of credit, currency conversion and the stability of foreign currencies, shipping terminology, and shipping methods.

Don't take this lightly. If you don't follow the right procedures, your shipment may be seized by overseas customs agents. If you don't arrange payment guarantees in advance, you may never get paid. If you don't word your sales and delivery contract correctly, your overseas buyer could find some technical loophole and refuse payment.

The U.S. government encourages exports, and has set up offices across the United States to help you with overseas sales. To find out more about export laws and procedures, log onto the Department of Commerce site **www.export.gov**. Contact the Bureau of Export Administration (the BXA): **www.bxa.doc.gov**. The U.S. Small Business Administration (the SBA) also offers help to businesses that want to export. The SBA has seventeen U.S. Export Assistance Centers across the U.S. Call 800-U-ASK-SBA or visit their Web sites **www.sba.gov** and **www.exim.gov**.

---

## Chapter 39:
# Complying With Foreign Laws

*"You may not realize it, but everyone from the World Trade Organization to the Commercial Court of Lille, France, to the tax collectors in Orland Park, Illinois, believes you are subject to their jurisdiction."*
**—Larry Downes, The Industry Standard Magazine**

Every country has its own laws governing Internet business. Some countries outlaw the sale of certain products. Some countries have laws governing the wording of guarantees, medical claims, even discounts. Several countries have strict privacy protection laws. Some countries simply don't want foreign businesses selling directly to their citizens.

If you make a sale to someone in, say, Italy, there is no telling if the Italian government will demand that you adhere to Italian laws. Already, the governments of both France and Germany have filed complaints against two large U.S. Internet businesses that violated laws in those countries.

There is no practical way for a small Web business to know the laws in other countries. Foreign laws are difficult to obtain and often near impossible to understand.

Some legal experts suggest that you make a reasonable "good faith" effort to learn about the laws of the countries you are doing business in. This may be particularly advisable if your Web site will generate significant sales from just a few countries. You may want to see if the countries have an Internet site, or you may want to actually contact the countries' consulates in the United States.

Check the many Web sites operated by the U.S. Department of Commerce. The Department of Commerce is at the forefront in the battles over international restrictions on Internet business. NAFTA (North American Free Trade Agreement) has wiped out many trade restrictions for doing business with Mexico and Canada. The World Trade Organization (and all of its police) are trying to break down international trade barriers all over the world.

One fight has been over privacy rights of Europeans who provide information to U.S. Web sites. The U.S. Department of Commerce has negotiated an agreement, called the "Safe Harbor Privacy Principles," with the countries that are part of the European Union. Any U.S. business that signs on to the agreement and follows the privacy rules spelled out in the agreement, will not be challenged by the countries in the European Union. For more information about the "safe harbor" rules, log onto **www.ita.doc.gov**.

Most Web businesses, however, simply take the overseas orders, ship the goods, and hope they don't get an unfriendly call from the KGB or the Ambassador from Egypt. So far, no small Internet business that I know of has had any trouble with international laws. As the French say, *Courage, mes amis*.

**"We've only begun to tap the vast potential of the Web to enhance our lives, by which I mean sell us stuff. You'll be able to order everything you see on the screen, from anywhere in the world, through your Internet account. This means that, merely by spilling beer on your keyboard, you could become legally obligated to purchase a helicopter."**

—*International Internet Consultant Dave Barry*

# Section Eight:
# Home Business

*"Image is everything."*

—Home Office Magazine

# Chapter 40:
# Home, Inc.

*"My home is corporate headquarters. The nerve center of our company is the laundry room. It houses the company's file server, fax machine, alarm system, credit card processing equipment, washer, and dryer. At night, with all the lights flashing, it looks like the deck of the Starship Enterprise."*
**—Glen Paul, Co-founder, QwikQuote Development**

Of the million-plus Internet businesses in the United States, the great majority are home based. The Internet economy is truly a home-business economy: someone in a spare bedroom, or out in the garage, or maybe an entire separate office with its own entrance and amenities.

Just about everyone now knows that Bill Hewlett and David Packard started their legendary company in Mr. Hewlett's garage. Steve Jobs started Apple Computer in his home, Bill Gates started Microsoft in his, Michael Dell Started Dell Computers in his. Ted Waitt started Gateway Computers in the family barn, as he often bragged about in his advertisements.

Computer geniuses are not alone in their proud boasts of starting from home. Mrs. Fields started her cookie business at home. Lillian Vernon started her mail order business at home. Walt Disney created Mickey and Donald and the Walt Disney Company at his kitchen table. William Harley and the Davidson brothers, Arthur and Walter, started their motorcycle business in a shed in the Davidson's backyard. And the Internet's most famous Web start-up, Amazon.com, was founded by Jeff Bezos in his home garage in Seattle.

The number of home-based businesses in the U.S., especially since the growth of the Internet, has increased tremendously in recent years. Dun & Bradstreet reports that 50% of *all* small businesses are now home-based. Inc. magazine reports that 50% of its "Inc. 500" businesses (the 500 fastest growing small businesses in the United States) started at home. The U.S. Department of the Census and the U.S. Bureau of Labor Statistics report that there are over ten million full-time home based businesses in the United States, and an additional nine million part-time and sideline home businesses. And despite the huge growth of Hewlett-Packard, Harley-Davidson, and a few other famous former home businesses, 80% of all businesses that start in the home stay there.

People who start businesses are often portrayed as "risk takers." But the smart new business owner is really just the opposite, what I call a "risk minimizer." A home-based business is the easiest and least risky way to test out your Internet business ideas and build your business at your own speed. A home business lets you start out part-time, evenings and weekends. You can keep your job, you don't have to refinance your home, you don't have to gamble your savings.

Every new business person makes mistakes. And some of those mistakes are going to cost you money. You charged too little. You paid too much. You said the wrong thing to the wrong person, and lost a customer. You forgot an important detail when agreeing to a job, and lost your shirt.

When you start at home, in your spare time, your mistakes are less costly than if you were going at it full time, with lots of overhead, bills to pay, can't afford any mistakes, a real pressure cooker. The start-slow-and-learn-as-you-go home business eliminates most of the pressure. You can learn from your mistakes. Your business can afford to make low-budget mistakes.

## Defining a Home Business

The term "home (or home-based) business" applies to anyone working for himself or herself, whose main business location is in the home or in a separate structure on the home property. The term "home business," and the laws specifically addressing home businesses, apply not just to businesses that buy and sell goods, but to home based inventors, contractors, professionals, freelancers, designers, consultants, Internet entrepreneurs, anyone who is self-employed.

Everything in this book applies to home businesses as well as businesses operated from a separate business location. But home businesses are also subject to government rules and restrictions, and income tax laws, that apply only to home-based businesses. Home businesses, just because they are in your home, have their own unique problems and rewards.

## The Good, The Bad, and the Family

When a business is in the home, constantly staring at you 24/7, people business owners tend to put in many more hours than they would if they had to get in the car and drive to the office. After dinner, early in the morning, the middle of the night. To do a slight rewrite of an old children's song, *"You wake up in the morning, it's a quarter to two / Wide awake, don't know what to do / You go to work / Do do do do do / You go to work."* It's life for a lot of home business owners.

More than in any other endeavor, a home business demands that you find a balance, that you make time for your family and for yourself. Successful home business owners set regular business hours, and stick to them—most of the time, anyway. At 5 pm, they turn off the phone, turn on the answering machine, lock the door to the office, and "go home."

But the opposite is also true. For some people, the special advantage of a home business is that they can work when the inspiration hits. The middle of dinner or the middle of the night is not off limits. The family, if they have a family, understands it, or tolerates it, or maybe hates it, but the bottom line is that it is your business. It will only be successful if you run it the way you want.

## Perception is Reality

Home business was once thought to be the poor stepchild of the small business world, a second-rate way to make a living. Part time hobbyists, stay-at-home parents, laid-off executives. Why aren't you good enough to have an office downtown?

Times and perceptions, fortunately, have changed. Many professionals and tradespeople work from their homes. Most Internet entrepreneurs work from their homes.

The old stereotype is fading. But it is not completely gone. Everything you do to help create an image of professionalism will help. Design professional looking stationery, business cards, brochures. Don't skimp. Create the image you want to convey.

If you do not want people dropping by your home unannounced, don't include your street address. Use a Post Office box or a private mail box (PMB) at a mail box store. Make sure the telephone directory does not list your home address.

If you are doing business 100% on the Internet, if all of your business contacts are through the Internet, none in person, the appearance of your home office is not important. But if your customers and clients will be coming to your home, you have a lot of work to do to make the business look professional, to separate it from the living part of your home, to make the entire home and surroundings look clean and prosperous. Wash the windows. Mow the lawn. Sweep the stairs. Little things add up. People do judge you by the clothes you wear. They judge your business the same way. Remember, you are your business. And now your home is also your business.

Privacy is extremely important to many people. They do not want to discuss their business or their finances with your family sitting nearby. If it is possible to have a separate entrance, neither you nor your clients need to deal with your living area. If you have animals, keep in mind that many people don't like animals. Many people are allergic to animal hair.

## The Business Telephone

If you want your customers to take you seriously, a dedicated business telephone line, answered as though it was a business and not the kitchen phone, is the first major step. Picking up the phone and saying "Hello" doesn't exactly sound professional. The customer is confused. "Is this, uh, is this a real business?"

If the business has a name, answer using the business name. If you are working as a self-employed professional, answer with your name. "Good morning, this is Hugo Hackenbush."

Many self employed individuals who use their own name as their business name, use their residential listing for their telephone. This may save you money, but it does not always work to your benefit. Telephone directories are separated between business and residential. A business listing will put you in the business section, which is where your clients expect to find you. A business listing also usually includes a free Yellow Pages listing. When you have a business listing, you can also include your name in the residential pages for a few extra dollars a month.

Customers don't expect business phones to be constantly busy. If you spend a lot of time on the phone, consider voice mail. Forget call waiting. I can't think of a faster way to lose clients than to put them through the call waiting routine.

If you do get voice mail, keep it short and sweet. Don't leave a long introduction, don't make your customers push buttons. And, for goodness sake, don't tell them that your call is important to us...

## Chapter 41:
# Home Business Basics

*"Place for most people is important, having a sense of structure, of belonging. Space is a way that people can psychologically divide their lives, so they have a life outside of their work. If you want your home office to be truly heavenly, make sure you can walk away from it."*
**—Sarah Edwards, co-author, "Working From Home"**

Just because corporate America defines an office as a claustrophobic cubicle doesn't mean you have to set up your own office as such. The luxury of a home office is that you can spread out wherever you want. And, often, the problem of a home office is that you can spread out wherever you want. When home and home office start overlapping, chaos starts creeping in. Running your business is confusing enough without the extra headache of nonbusiness paperwork shuffled into the deck.

The first rule for a successful home-based Internet business: keep your business and your personal life as separate as possible. When you are working from home, it is too easy to mingle personal and businesses expenses, equipment, cash, paperwork, and everything else. The result is inaccurate business records, inaccurate tax returns, and a lot of wasted time sorting out what's business and what's personal.

I can tell you, from years of business experience, from being involved with several hundred small businesses of all types, that possibly the most important secret to business survival is, believe it or not, organization. Disorganized people have a terrible time managing a business.

If at all possible, have a separate room, or at least a separate area, desk, files and shelves, dedicated to business and nothing else. The simple act of physical separation will make your office more organized, your business more manageable, your life more sane. Most studies have shown that people who mix residential space with work space tend to become disenchanted with working at home. If the kids need a computer to do their homework, buy a second one and put it someplace else.

Remember the predictions a few years ago about the "paperless office?" The computer and then the Internet were supposed to eliminate most of the paperwork in a business. Files would be easier to store and access. The exact opposite has happened. Businesses have more paper than ever. Faxes. Photocopies. Ink jet printers. Post-It notes falling off of everything. Having your files organized in a file cabinet or on your computer, having a system that lets you locate files quickly, will make your business more manageable, and will save you a great deal of time, hunting down lost paperwork.

*Linda Blair Design, Scarsdale, N.Y.*

The more office equipment you have, the more electricity you'll be using. If you find you are overloading your home circuits, tripping circuit breakers, you may need to get an electrician to help rewire the house. Or you may not need any rewiring. You may only need to reconfigure where equipment is plugged in. Different electrical outlets in the same room may be on different circuits, enabling you to break up the current draw. If you know where the circuit breakers are for your house, you can shut off one breaker at a time, and see which wall outlets are wired to which circuit breakers. You could run your computer off of one circuit, the electric heater off another, avoiding current overload.

## Zoning

Home businesses are often subject to restrictive zoning laws. Zoning laws vary considerably from one location to another. Some communities outlaw home businesses entirely (though that has rarely stopped a determined home-based operator from setting up quietly and clandestinely). Some communities restrict the type of business that can be operated out of a home, the size of home businesses, the number of employees, number of visitors, the amount of inventory on hand, number of vehicles, parking, signage, even the hours of operation. Some communities allow home businesses in the residence but not in a freestanding garage or shop on the property. Some communities, hallelujah, have no restrictions whatsoever.

For specific zoning regulations, contact city hall if you are in city limits, or contact county offices if you are outside city limits. Don't tell them who you are; just ask if there are zoning restrictions on home businesses. And don't rely on verbal information. Get a copy of the written law, and read it. If certain types of home business are allowed, find out exactly what types of businesses are and are not allowed. Try to define your business to meet the zoning requirements. Sometimes all you have to do is get the terminology right.

Before you get totally bogged down in zoning prohibitions, you should consider the reasons for zoning laws. People do not want noise, odors, trash, traffic, parking problems and strangers near their homes. They want quiet and peaceful residential neighborhoods. So they banish businesses, which often bring noise, traffic and strangers, to other areas of the community.

But the typical Internet business is invisible: no signs, quiet, few if any customers or employees. Such a business is not likely to disturb neighbors, and you are not likely to get in trouble with the zoning authorities, even if you are technically breaking the law. Zoning officials don't go snooping around looking for violations. They usually act only when they receive a complaint.

The first and foremost zoning law, in my opinion, is: Be Considerate Of Your Neighbors. Put yourself in their situation. How would you feel if a neighbor started a business like the one you plan to start? If it seems appropriate to you, talk to your neighbors about your plans. Find out, before you start your business, if there will be opposition or bad feelings.

Find ways to minimize the impact of your business on the neighborhood. If you will be having several people come for a conference, consider renting a small back room in a local restaurant instead. If you receive or ship a lot of packages, consider using a mailbox store for pick up and drop off of packages. Have a parking space in front of your home or on your driveway for visitors. Keep signs small and tasteful; a small plaque next to the door may be all you need. Consider renting storage space for your inventory.

What happens if you are operating a home business, and you suddenly receive a visit from an official of the zoning board, advising you that you are breaking the law? Ask if a complaint has been filed, and if so, why? Are you causing a genuine nuisance? Will the zoning people allow you to alter your practices to eliminate the nuisance? Can you request a waiver, a variance or a special use permit that will allow you to continue in business?

A public hearing is part of the variance application in most cities. If any neighbors show up to oppose the variance at that hearing, your chances are pretty much shot. So it is a good idea to get on friendly terms with your neighbors, and let them know just what you are doing before you apply for a variance. Your neighbors might help by writing letters or signing a petition in support of your business.

## Landlords, Condominiums, Co-ops and Homeowners Associations

A bigger problem than zoning regulations are residence contracts. If you rent your home, live in a condo or co-op, or live in some type of restricted housing development, be sure the lease, ownership agreement or real estate covenant does not prohibit a home business. Co-ops in particular often have strictly-enforced restrictions on home businesses.

No one will likely be spying on you. If you are quiet, not troubling your neighbors, chances are you could operate an Internet business undetected and unharrassed just about anywhere. Most rules are ignored, aren't they? As one famous former politician said, "Don't ask, don't tell."

## Insurance

Home owner's and home renter's insurance probably does not cover your home-based business, and does not provide liability protection if someone, visiting your home on business, is injured. If a customer, supplier, delivery person, employee, contractor, or any business-related person is injured, you may wind up with a lawsuit and medical expenses. Your insurance carrier may not only refuse to pay a claim, the insurance company may terminate your coverage.

Don't keep your home business a secret from your insurance company. Talk to your insurance agent about your home business. If you use a separate building, such as a garage or barn, for an office or storage or other business use, mention this to your insurance agent. Some policies cover only the residence itself.

For home-based businesses independent professionals, there are two types of home business insurance available to you: endorsements, and in-home business policies.

**Endorsements:** If your business is a small office type of business, low income, no employees, few if any customers coming to your office, and a low dollar value for equipment and inventory, you may be able to add an endorsement (also called a "rider") to your existing home owner or home renter policy. The additional premium is usually very low. Such an endorsement usually covers liability, damage to the building, and a small amount of coverage to business assets. For many small Internet businesses, this endorsement may be all the insurance you'll ever need.

**In-Home Business Policies:** If your home business is a primary source of income, or if you have employees or customers coming to your house, or if you have valuable equipment or inventory you want to insure, you probably will need what's called an "In-Home Business Policy." This is a separate policy from your regular homeowner policy. It offers coverage for businesses that exceed the limits on homeowner endorsements. In-home policies often include liability coverage, damage to the building, coverage of business assets, and sometimes business interruption insurance, which will pay you for lost earnings if you are unable to operate your business because of damage to your home. These different types of insurance are covered in more detail in **Chapter 11: Insurance**. You will need to purchase regular homeowners insurance in addition to the in-home business policy.

## Where to Find Insurance

If your current home insurance company is not receptive to your needs, look elsewhere. Some insurance companies do not want to insure home businesses, but some insurers are eager to insure home businesses. Trade organizations and professional societies sometimes also offer home-business insurance. Insurance policies, and rates, vary from company to company.

Be sure you are dealing with a reputable and financially stable company. If you are not familiar with the company, contact your state's insurance commissioner. Find out if the company is licensed to do business in your state and if there are any problems with the company.

Finally, read your insurance policy. Don't just accept the insurance agent's word, verify it. If the language of the policy is confusing, or if it seems to contradict with the agent told you, take the policy to your agent and sit down and discuss it. Your home, your business, and your money are all at stake. Know what is covered.

## Insurance: Employees

If you have employees, your insurance needs multiply. Home business policies do not include provisions for employees. Regular liability insurance, which provides medical coverage for your customers and business visitors if they are injured, does not cover employees. You will need worker's compensation insurance for employees, which is required by law in most states (see **Chapter 11: Insurance**). Family employees are often exempt from workers compensation insurance and also from regular employment laws and taxes.

If you have medical insurance for your family, you should check with your insurance carrier about coverage of family members working in the family business. If a family member is injured while working, is he or she covered?

If you hire independent contractors, self-employed individuals, to do work for your business—maybe a bookkeeper who comes in once a month, or a cleaning person, or someone to fix your computer—these people are not employees. They are not covered by Workers Compensation insurance. If an independent contractor is injured while on your premises, your liability coverage, the coverage you have for customers and business visitors, should cover the contractor.

## Safe Workplace

Even if you are fully insured for personal liability, make sure your home business is safe for visitors. Business customers and clients will not be forgiving of a spill that makes them slip and fall, or an obstacle that makes them trip. Even if you don't get sued, you'll lose a customer for sure.

Keep walkways well lit. Check for icy paths, slippery steps, obstacles underfoot, loose rugs. If there is an unexpected step up or step down, post a warning. If there are sliding glass doors, put some decal or decoration on the glass so someone doesn't walk right into it. Tie up the dog.

# Chapter 42:
# Income Tax Laws For Home Businesses

*"The home based business is the last refuge from the bureaucratic meddling and stifling protectionism that inevitably accompany any and all government involvement. Those who long for government action on their behalf should remember the axiom, For every government action, there is an overwhelming and destructive reaction."*
**—Business owner Norman D. Wood**

When it comes to reporting and paying income taxes, the Internal Revenue Service treats home businesses just like every other business. The "Income Tax" part of **Chapter 29: Taxes** applies to your business no matter where it is located.

There are several income tax laws that apply only to home businesses. They are explained here. But keep in mind that tax laws change every year. Every time some congressman gets bored, the first thing he wants to do is change the income tax laws. Do not rely on the tax information in this book until you verify it with the IRS or a competent tax accountant.

## Profit or Loss From a Home Business

You compute the profit or loss from your home business the same way you would for any business, with a few important exceptions (covered in this chapter).

A profitable home business will increase your taxes. If your home Internet business is a moonlight operation—that is, if you also hold a job as an employee working for someone else—the income or loss from the home business is added to the wages from your employment, along with any other income such as bank interest, in determining your taxable income.

If your home business shows a loss, as some businesses do when just getting started, you can use that loss to offset your wages (and your other income) in determining your taxable income and figuring your taxes. The business loss will reduce your income taxes, a consolation prize of sorts.

But you're losing money, and if you don't know why, it's time to stop and figure out why. You need to determine whether you can turn the business around or whether you should pack it in, and try something else. "Businesses always lose money the first year" is not a good answer, and isn't true. If you are puzzled, get help. Hire an accountant for an hour's worth of advice. It will be worth every penny.

## The "Home Office" Deduction

This is the biggest and most problematical home-business tax law. This is one of the few tax laws that you really should understand thoroughly. A lot of money—your money—is at stake.

The term "Home Office," for this important tax law, refers to any home business space—office, workshop, studio, warehouse, store, showroom, etc.—and the expenses directly related to the space including utilities, insurance, mortgage interest, property taxes, home repairs, etc. The term "home" includes a house, apartment, loft, condominium, trailer, mobile home, or boat (if you are living on it). The term also includes any separate structure that is part of your residence such as a garage, shop or other building.

In order to deduct your home office expenses, you must meet some very specific rules. These rules apply to sole proprietors, partners, owners of S corporation, and members (owners) of Limited Liability Companies.

Failure to qualify for the home office deduction doesn't prohibit you from operating your business out of your home. It only means that one possibly large expense is not deductible on your federal income taxes. You can still deduct all legitimate business expenses other than those directly related to the business space itself.

**C Corporations:** The home-office rules do not apply to C corporations. You can skip this entire chapter. If you own a C corporation and work out of your home, you have two ways to deduct your office expenses. You can take a personal tax deduction as an employee business expense, if you are eligible and if you itemize deductions on Schedule A of your 1040 return. Or you can lease the office to the corporation, at which time you as an individual have rental income to report on your personal tax return.

## Regular and Exclusive Use

To be eligible for the home office deduction, a specific part of your home must be used regularly and exclusively for business. It can be a separate room or even part of a room as long as it is used for the business and nothing else. Period. No television in the room. No personal paperwork at the desk. (No games on the computer?) It can't double as a guest room, or kid's play room, or anything else, even when you are not working.

If you are using part of a room for your business, block it off with a partition, or a bookcase or file cabinet. This way you have a clean delineation of where the business space begins and ends. Should you ever be audited, you can much more easily defend you home-office deduction.

One exception to the exclusive rule: If your home is your sole fixed location for a retail sales business and if you regularly store your inventory in your home, the expense of maintaining the storage area is deductible even if it isn't exclusive use of the space.

## Principal Place of Business

In addition to the Regular and Exclusive Use rules, your home office must meet at least one of three requirements:

1. The office must be your principal place of business. "Principal place of business" is defined by the IRS as "the most important, consequential, or influential location." For home Internet businesses, your home is probably your only place of business, so it meets this requirement, and you can skip #2 and #3. You've met the IRS requirement.

2. The office must be used regularly (not just occasionally) by customers, clients, or patients, or to generate sales.

3. The office must be the sole fixed location where you conduct most of your administrative or management activities for the business: where you do your paperwork, or your research, or ordering supplies, or scheduling appointments.

Meeting any one of the three above requirements qualifies you for a home office deduction (as long as you also meet the Regular Use and Exclusive Use tests). You can have a separate "principal place of business" for each trade or business you operate.

## What's Deductible

Deductible home-office expenses include a percentage of your rent if you rent your home, or a percentage of the depreciation if you own your home; and an equal percentage of utilities, garbage pickup, property tax, mortgage interest and insurance. Minor home repairs are deductible. Major repairs must be depreciated.

The best way to figure percentage of the home eligible for the home-office deduction is to measure square footage. If 20% of the square footage is used exclusively for business, then 20% of the rent can be deducted, or 20% of the cost of the house (land excluded) can be depreciated, and 20% of home utilities, insurance, taxes, maintenance, etc. can be deducted.

Business owners can also calculate business use of the home based on a room count, but unless all rooms are the same size, you will not get an accurate percentage to deduct. You may be cheating yourself, or you may be cheating the IRS, by saying one room in five equals a 20% deduction.

If your homeowner's insurance includes special coverage or additional premiums just for the business, the business coverage is 100% deductible as a business expense. The balance of the homeowner's insurance, the coverage that applies to the entire home, is prorated, based on the percentage of the home used for business.

You can also take a 100% deduction for decorating and for cleaning the office area, and for furniture, equipment, and office machines for the office. If you install a security system, you can deduct or depreciate the full cost if the system is just for the business area; or you can deduct a percentage of the cost if the system is for the entire house.

One thing you cannot deduct is landscaping around your home, even if the landscaping was done solely to enhance the appearance of your business. The only exception to this rule is for home-based landscapers and gardeners, if they are using the landscaping as an example of their work.

## Warning: Two Tax Traps for Homeowners

Here is a very important warning for homeowners. If you are eligible for the home-office deduction, you will run into two serious tax complications when you sell your house.

Tax Trap Number One: Homeowners who claim a deduction for a home business are allowed to depreciate—that is, write off—a portion of the cost of the home every year, as explained above. But when you sell your home, any depreciation you were allowed must be "recaptured." This means you must add up all the depreciation you were eligible for during all the years you had a home office—*whether you took the depreciation or not*—and pay income tax on that depreciation when you sell the house. This can bring a large and most unpleasant tax bill the year of sale.

Tax Trap Number Two: You are probably aware of the huge tax break for people when they sell their homes. They don't have to pay income tax on the profit, up to as much as $500,000. But if you are deducting a home office, when you sell your home, the office portion of the home is not eligible for the tax-free exclusion. If you sell the house at a profit, you will owe taxes on the portion of the home that is your office.

You can avoid Tax Trap Number Two. If you were not eligible for a home office deduction for at least two of the five years prior to sale, you don't have to exclude the office portion of your home from the tax-free gain. Your entire home will be considered a residence. So if you know you will be selling your home in the near future, be sure that at least two years prior to the sale you make your home office ineligible for the home office deduction, such as no longer using it exclusively for business.

The two-out-of-five-years rule, however, does NOT apply to Tax Trap Number One, the problem of recaptured depreciation when you sell the house. There is no way to avoid this tax bill other than making sure, right from the first day you start your business, that your home business is not eligible for the home office deduction (such as being sure it flunks the "exclusive use" test).

These laws are confusing, but they are important issues that can have a major impact on your bank account. You should discuss these tax laws with your accountant before you claim a home office deduction.

## Business Loss

If your home business shows a loss, part of your home office expenses are not deductible this year. You may deduct regular business expenses (other than expenses for the office space itself) and may deduct a percentage of interest and property taxes on the office, regardless of profit or loss. But the remaining home office expenses—including rent or depreciation, insurance, utilities, maintenance—may be deducted this year only to the extent there is no loss.

Expenses you cannot deduct because of this limitation can be carried forward to futures years, and written off against future years' profits.

## The Home Office Deduction and IRS Audits

There is a widespread fear that taking a home-office deduction will greatly increase your chance of being audited by the IRS. This is a home-business myth that's been repeated over and over. It is not true. The home-office deduction itself does not increase your chance of an audit. A *large* home office deduction coupled with low income will, yes, increase your chance of an audit, the IRS being suspicious that maybe this isn't really a business. But even then, you odds of being audited are under 5%. If you are entitled to a home-office deduction (and if you won't have problems with the tax traps explained above) I suggest you take the deduction. If the U.S. Government in its wisdom is allowing a deduction, you in your wisdom should take it.

To file for the Home Office Deduction, you must fill out Form 8829, "Expenses for Business Use of Your Home." For more information, see IRS Publication #587, "Business Use of Your Home." The publication is free from any IRS office, or you can call the IRS toll free at 800-829-3676 and have them mail you a copy, or you can log onto the IRS's Web site **www.irs.gov** and download a copy.

## Two More Home-Business Tax Deductions

**Telephone.** The IRS has special tax rules for home-business telephones. You may not deduct the basic monthly rate for the first telephone line into your home. For tax purposes, it does not matter to the IRS how the phone is listed, business or personal, or how it is used. The basic rate for the first line into your home is not deductible even if it is listed and used as a business phone.

Expenses beyond the basic rate, such as business-related long distance calls, optional services, and any special business equipment, are deductible. Any additional lines into the house after the first line are fully deductible, if used exclusively for business.

**Business Mileage.** Business owners can deduct the cost of driving around town on business. You can take actual expenses, or you can take a flat rate of 34½¢ per mile for each business mile you drive (2001 rate; the rate changes from year to year).

The IRS does not allow a travel deduction for commuting. Regular commuting mileage, home to work and back, is not deductible. Home business owners do not commute, so this is not a problem, except for one fine point in the law.

If you drive around town visiting clients, the IRS considers the trip to your first client a commute, not deductible. The same goes for the trip home from your last call of the day. Any other local business travel is deductible.

There may be a way to avoid this loss of a deduction. If you go to your home office and do some work before you visit your first client, most accountants feel that you already did your commute (to your home office), and that your first client visit is deductible. Ditto for returning home after visiting your last client, if you return to your home office to work before quitting for the day. Pretty picky rules here, I admit. Part of the secret to success in business is (1) knowing the rules, and (2) knowing how to break them.

More tax deductions for driving: If you are taking classes or seminars related to your business, the mileage you drive to and from the classes is deductible.

The full details of the business mileage deduction are explained in IRS

Publication #463, "Travel, Entertainment, Gift, and Car Expenses." Free from any IRS office, or by calling toll free 800-829-3676, or on the Internet **www.irs.gov**.

## Chapter 43:
# Outgrowing the Home

*"It's hard to work when your kids are at home. You want to be with them. They want you. Or they want pizza. What are you going to do? You can't stick them in front of a video for more than 22 consecutive hours."*

**—Peggy Kalb, "Work and Family," Wall Street Journal**

The great majority of successful home businesses never leave home. The home-business owners manage to balance growth, making a living, and keeping a physically small space.

But many businesses finally decides that it's time to move out of the home and rent a commercial business location. Resistance from customers and clients, who don't feel comfortable working with a home operation, is occasionally a reason. Zoning problems sometimes cannot be solved. Growing families sometimes cramp the space. The need to put a clear distinction between your business and your personal life can be a powerful motivator to move the business out of the home.

The main reason most home businesses move out of the home is because the business grew to a point where the home could no longer hold it. More products to store, more room to work, more employees. Success is forcing you in a new direction. "Forcing" is hopefully too strong a word. Hopefully, your success is happily leading you in that new direction.

If you are, in truth, being "forced" to move when you'd much rather stay home, give serious thought to how you can restructure your business so that it can stay within the confines of your home and still be successful. Do you really need to add new products? Do you need more clients? Can you outsource some of the repetitive clerical work to another business, maybe someone working out of his or her home?

Before making a final decision whether or not to move out of the home, be sure you've figured all of the added expenses involved. Whether you bring in a single extra dollar or not, when you move the business out of the home, you will be paying addition expenses for: Moving costs. Rent or lease, and possibly rent deposits. Fixing up the new premises. Insurance. Utilities and telephone, including hook up fees and deposits. Security system. Outside cleaning and maintenance. City permits. Commuting expenses. And possibly other fixed costs.

Can your current income support those additional expenses? Or will you feel the pressure to have to bring in additional income that you may or may not be able to generate? You will have to deal with landlords, neighboring businesses, traffic and parking, neighborhood problems, civic responsibilities, the list sometimes seems endless. Are you sure you want to move out?

**Remember, the goal is to work at home, not to feel like you live at work.**

—*Jacqueline Lynn, Business Start-Ups Magazine*

# We've Only Just Begun

This is not just the title of a song, it is the real story of the Internet. The unfinished revolution.

Internet technology will keep improving. The current technology is still quite crude. For too many people, using a computer is like going to a movie theater and having to watch the projector instead of the movie. Internet technology will evolve until it is as flawless, and as invisible, as the telephone and the television. People will use the Web without having to struggle with computers and arcane codes.

Internet business remains on an intense learning curve, as it continues to define itself. There are lots of people doing things for the first time. The evolving business model is the critical issue for Internet businesses: the interaction between business and customer, between Web site and visitor, the changes in technology, and the changes in the laws governing Web commerce.

The game is afoot, Dr. Watson, and business will never be the same again. The Internet is the greatest business transformation of our lifetime. Keeping up is not a choice. It is a requirement for survival.

**It is not the strongest species that survive nor the most intelligent, but the most responsive to change.**
*—Charles Darwin*

# Government Web Addresses

## General Federal Government Assistance
U.S. Business Advisor: www.business.gov
U.S. Government Access Site: www.firstgov.gov
Federal Information Network: www.fedworld.gov

## Small Business Assistance
SCORE (Service Corps of Retired Executives): www.score.org
Small Business Administration: www.sba.gov
Small Business Development Centers: www.sba.gov/sbdc

## Major Federal Agencies
Census: www.census.gov
Department of Commerce: www.doc.gov
Department of Labor: www.dol.gov
Department of Transportation: www.dot.gov
Environmental Protection Agency: www.epa.gov
Federal Communications Commission: www.fcc.gov
Federal Trade Commission: www.ftc.gov
Food and Drug Administration: www.fda.gov
Government Printing Office: www.gpo.gov
Immigration & Naturalization Service: www.ins.usdoj.gov
Internal Revenue Service: www.irs.gov
Occupational Safety and Health Administration: www.osha.gov
Postal Service (Post Office): www.usps.com

## Copyright, Patent and Trademark Offices
Copyright Office: www.lcweb.loc.gov/copyright
Trademark Office: www.uspto.gov
Trademark Search: tess.uspto.gov (do not type www in the address)
Patent Office: www.uspto.gov
Patent Application: www.uspto.gov/ebc/index.html

## Importing and Exporting
Bureau of Export Administration: www.bxa.doc.gov
Customs Service: www.customs.gov
Department of Commerce: www.doc.gov; www.export.gov
Export Assistance Centers: www.sba.gov
Export Counseling Division: www.doc.gov
Export Import Bank: www.exim.gov
International Trade Administration: www.ita.doc.gov
International Trade Commission: www.usitc.gov
Office of International Trade: www.sba.gov/OIT
Overseas Private Investment Corporation: www.opic.gov
Small Business Administration: www.sba.gov
U.S. Trade and Development Agency: www.tda.gov
U.S. Trade Representative: www.ustr.gov
Safe Harbor Information: www.ita.doc.gov

## Non-Functioning Domain Names
If any of the above Web sites are not functioning, you can find the correct domain name for all Federal government agencies at one or both of these sites:

www.firstgov.gov
www.fedworld.gov

## State Government Web Addresses
For your state government's main Web site:

www.state.[your state's two-letter abbreviation].us

# Index

# Quality Small Business Books & Software from Bell Springs Publishing

---

*26th Edition:*
## Small Time Operator:
### How to Start Your Own Business, Keep Your Books, Pay Your Taxes & Stay Out of Trouble
Bernard Kamoroff, C.P.A.

Be Your Own Boss. Here is the help you need to take control of your life and be a success, on your own terms. For all businesses and self-employed individuals, here—in an all-new, fully revised and expanded edition—is complete, up-to-date information:

Getting all your permits & licenses. How to finance your business. Finding the right business location. Creating & using a business plan. Choosing & protecting your business name. How to set up a complete yet simple bookkeeping system. Do you need to incorporate? Hiring employees. Buying a business or franchise. Federal, state & local taxes. Internet businesses. Dealing with—and avoiding!—the IRS. Insurance, contracts, pricing, trademarks...and much more.
With 600,000 copies in print, *Small Time Operator* has sold more copies than any other business start-up guide ever published.

**#02**   224 pages, paperback, 8½"x11"                                    **$16.95**

---

*Third Edition:*
## 422 Tax Deductions
### for Businesses and Self-Employed Individuals
Bernard Kamoroff, C.P.A.

You get a raise every time you find a legitimate tax deduction. Here are 422 of them:

♦ Deductions you never heard about.
♦ Deductions your accountant forgot to ask you about.
♦ Deductions your software program got wrong.
♦ Deductions the IRS chose not to list on their tax forms.

Are you paying more taxes than you have to? The IRS is not going to tell you about a deduction you failed to take, and your tax accountant is not likely to take the time to ask you about every deduction you're entitled to.
It's up to you. The savings can be tremendous.

**#03**   224 pages, paperback, 7"x9"                                       **$17.95**

## Marketing Without Advertising
Michael Phillips & Salli Rasberry

Does advertising work? Do you need to advertise? Are there better ways to market your business?

The first part of this startling book argues convincingly and with documented proof that almost all advertising is totally ineffective and an utter waste of money; and that most business owners have been successfully duped into believing that advertising is both necessary and productive in spite of obvious evidence to the contrary.

*Marketing Without Advertising* is much more than an argument against advertising. Packed into this little gem of a book are more than a hundred tried and tested marketing strategies that have worked for all kinds of small businesses. Here is what you need to know to successfully promote your business—at little or no cost.

Possibly the last $19 you'll ever spend on advertising!

**#04**   185 pages, paperback, 7"x9"                              **$18.95**

---

## Free Help From Uncle Sam
### To Start or Expand Your Business
William Alarid & Gustav Berle

Here, in one convenient source, are several hundred government programs and agencies that purchase from small businesses and that offer services, publications and financial assistance to small businesses:

Government loan programs and financial incentives. Import and export assistance. Census information and statistics. Special programs for women, minorities and handicapped people. Free small business information and counseling. State by state listings for Federal Information Centers, SBA field offices, International Trade Administration offices, Small Business Development Centers, and each state's Small Business Assistance program and offices.

Includes a list of government agencies that purchase from small businesses, and explains how you can sell your goods and services to these agencies.

**#05**   233 pages, paperback, 5½"x8½"                          **$17.95**

---

## Basic Guide to
## Selling Arts & Crafts
James Dillehay

Artists and craftspeople can fine tune their business, and novices can learn how to turn a hobby into a livelihood: Product lines. Wholesaling. Consignment. Displays. Shows. Pricing. Discounts. Dealing with show promoters, sales reps, store and gallery owners. Finding sales outlets. Licensing. And more.

This is the Official Training Guide used by the American Crafters Guild and the Association of Creative Crafts. The author is on the Advisory Board of the National Craft Association.

**#06**   220 pages, paperback, 6"x9"                              **$14.95**

## Small Time Operator: The Software
Bernard Kamoroff CPA, Steve Steinke & Emil Krause

For people with a spreadsheet program, here is the same bookkeeping system as the one in *Small Time Operator*, on a ready-to-use spreadsheet file (template). The disk contains 23 spreadsheets: Income and Expenditure ledgers. Profit and loss statement. Balance Sheet. Payroll. Cash Flow. Net worth. Petty cash. Partners' capital. Credit ledger. Inventory control. Business plan. Invoice form. Mailing list. Loan amortization. Telephone-address file. Includes 184-page manual.

    **This is not a stand-alone program. You *must* have** Excel, Lotus 1-2-3, Quattro Pro, or Works spreadsheet program. (PC only. Not available on Macintosh.)

**#07**   184 page manual and disk                        **$29.95**


## We Own It:
## Starting & Managing Cooperatives and Employee Owned Businesses
Peter Honigsberg, Attorney at Law & Bernard Kamoroff, C.P.A.

The only book of its kind, *We Own It* gives you the legal, tax and management information you need to start and operate all types of consumer, producer and worker co-ops. Covers non-profit, for-profit and cooperative corporations, ESOP's, and all other options.

**#08**   150 pages, paperback, 8½"x11"                     **$14.00**


## Getting Into The Mail Order Business
Julian L. Simon

Everything you need to know to get started and be a success in mail order:
    The kinds of products that naturally sell well in mail order, and those that don't. How to locate and test your market and promote your products. Selling through catalogs. How *not* to compete with the large mail order houses. How to create mail order copy that works.
    And more: Setting up shop. Where to go for direct mail lists. Handling shipping, refunds, guarantees. How the mail order laws affect your business.
    The most successful mail-order book ever published: in print for over 20 years!

**#09**   291 pages, paperback, 6"x9"                        **$14.95**


## Negotiating the Purchase or Sale of a Business
James C. Comiskey

This thorough guide will help a buyer determine if a business is worth buying. How profitable the business presently is. How good are the location and the lease. How easy or hard will it be for a new owner to take over. How much to expect to pay. How to value the inventory and assets. How much to pay for "goodwill".
    This guide will help the seller determine a fair asking price, prepare for the sale, and deal with prospective buyers. Includes legal and tax aspects of a sale, the contract, & common financing arrangements.

**#10**   137 pages, 40 worksheets, paperback, 8½"x11"            **$18.95**

## Starting Young
Joe Mellin

Sixteen year old Joe Mellin is not only a great business-kid (he started and successfully operated three after-school businesses), he's an excellent writer as well, explaining in this concise guide how any kid with an idea and a little go get 'em can start your own business, have fun, and earn real money. Forget begging your parents for an allowance, get this book and live life like a king.

**#11**   108 pages, paperback, 6"x9"                                          **$12.00**


## Selling To Uncle Sam
C.L. Crownover & M. Henricks

Find out how you can join the many businesses successfully selling to our government, how to get your company on the government's select bid list, how to maneuver through the rules and red tape. It's work, but it's worth it!

**#12**   205 pages, hardback, 6"x9"                                          **$17.95**


## Marketing Myths
K.J. Clancy & R.S. Shulman

Marketing—spreading the word about your product or service—is essential to *every* business, big or small. Here is the help you need to cut through the theories and myths, and deal with the real world of finding and keeping customers and clients. **#13**   309 pages, hardback,  6"x9"                      **$19.95**


## The Entrepreneurial PC
Bernard J. David

A hundred businesses you can start using word processing, desktop publishing, online information research, database marketing, e-mail, computer graphics, and accounting, bookkeeping and payroll programs.

**#14**   294 pages, hardback, 7"x9"                                          **$17.95**


## Legal Help for Your Business
Mead Hedglon

Save both your money and your sanity in dealing with legal matters: when you don't need lawyers, how to avoid litigation, and if necessary, how to get the best help at the lowest possible cost.

**#15**   296 pages, hardback, 6"x9"                                          **$16.95**


## Golden Entrepreneuring
James B. Arkebauer

A "golden" wealth of tips and ideas to use your years and experience to your advantage. Real, hands-on help for those of you fed up with the corporate struggle or bored with retirement, and looking to have some fun—and make some money

**#16**   254 pages, paperback, 6"x9"                                         **$16.95**

*Support Your Local Bookstore.*
*Online Operator* is available in bookstores across the country. If you are
unable to locate it, or any of our other titles, please order directly from us.

## *Our Guarantee:*
All Bell Springs books and software are fully guaranteed. If you are not satisfied for any reason, return the items for a full refund, no questions asked.

## *In A Hurry?*
Call Toll Free **1-800-515-8050**, or fax your order to **707-459-8614**. We accept
MasterCard, VISA, Discover, American Express. We usually ship same day.

------------------------------------------------------------------------

# BELL SPRINGS PUBLISHING
Mail Order Sales Dept.
Box 1240, Willits, California 95490

| | | | |
|---|---|---|---|
| ____ #01 | Online Operator | $18.95 | _____ |
| ____ #02 | Small Time Operator | $16.95 | _____ |
| ____ #03 | 422 Tax Deductions | $17.95 | _____ |
| ____ #04 | Marketing Without Advertising | $18.95 | _____ |
| ____ #05 | Free Help from Uncle Sam | $17.95 | _____ |
| ____ #06 | Selling Arts & Crafts | $14.95 | _____ |
| ____ #07 | Small Time Operator Software | $29.95 | _____ |
| ____ #08 | We Own It | $14.00 | _____ |
| ____ #09 | Getting Into Mail Order | $14.95 | _____ |
| ____ #10 | Purchase or Sale of Business | $18.95 | _____ |
| ____ #11 | Starting Young | $12.00 | _____ |
| ____ #12 | Selling to Uncle Sam | $17.95 | _____ |
| ____ #13 | Marketing Myths | $19.95 | _____ |
| ____ #14 | Entrepreneurial PC | $17.95 | _____ |
| ____ #15 | Legal Help | $16.95 | _____ |
| ____ #16 | Golden Entrepreneuring | $16.95 | _____ |

**Book Total**       $ _____
California residents add 7% sales tax    _____
Shipping       $    **3.00**
***Total:*** check, money order or credit card    $ _____

Name_____

Address_____

City _____ State _____ Zip _____

Credit Card # _____ Exp. Date _____

Signature_____